jB
VAN
ELL
12/89

Ellis, Rafaela

Martin Van Buren,
8th president of
the United States

117357

$12.95

DATE			

AR
BL: 9.6
pts: 5.0

© THE BAKER & TAYLOR CO.

Martin Van Buren

8th President of the United States

Martin Van Buren

8th President of the United States

Rafaela Ellis

 GARRETT EDUCATIONAL CORPORATION

Van

Cover: *Official presidential portrait of Martin Van Buren by George P. A. Healy.* (Copyrighted by the White House Historical Association; photograph by the National Geographic Society.)

Manufactured in the United States of America

Edited and produced by Synthegraphics Corporation

Library of Congress Cataloging in Publication Data

Ellis, Rafaela.
  Martin Van Buren, 8th president of the United States.

  (Presidents of the United States)
  Bibliography: p.
  Includes index.
  Summary: Traces the childhood, education, employment, political career, and presidency of man from Kinderhook, New York.
    1. Van Buren, Martin, 1782–1862—Juvenile literature.
  2. Presidents—United States—Biography—Juvenile literature. [1. Van Buren, Martin, 1782–1862.
  2. Presidents.] I. Title. II. Title: Martin Van Buren, eighth president of the United States. III. Series.
  E387.E48   1989   973.5'7'0924—dc19   [B]   [92]
  88-24535
  ISBN 0-944483-12-7

Contents

Chronology for Martin Van Buren

1782   Born on December 5 in Kinderhook, NY

1797– 1802   Read law with a local attorney

1803   Admitted to the New York State bar

1807   Married Hannah Hoes on February 21

1808   Appointed surrogate of Columbia County, New York

1812   Elected to the New York State Senate

1816   Appointed attorney general of New York

1819   Hannah Hoes Van Buren died

1821– 1828   Served in the U.S. Senate

1828   Elected governor of New York

1829   Chosen by President Andrew Jackson to be U.S. secretary of state

1832– 1837   Served as Vice-President under President Andrew Jackson

1837– 1841   Served as 8th President of the United States

1840   Defeated in bid for re-election

1848   Ran for President on the Free Soil Party ticket; was defeated

1862   Died on July 24

This mezzotint engraving of President Martin Van Buren was made by John Sartain, after a painting by Henry Inman. (Library of Congress.)

Chapter 1

The Rise of "Little Van"

The jurors who sat in the Kinderhook, New York, court-room were familiar with the young man who stood before them. Kinderhook was a small town, and everybody knew everybody else. Each of the 12 men charged with reaching a verdict in the case had long heard about young Mat Van Buren, the tavern-keeper's son.

For the past few years, Mat Van Buren had been study-ing law under Francis Silvester, one of the town's most able attorneys. But the boy was only 17, a long way from the 21 years of age required to practice law in the state of New York. So it was highly irregular to see him in the courtroom now, preparing to sum up a case before the jury.

Young Van Buren had a reputation for being wise and clever beyond his years. Today, that reputation would be put to the test as he faced a most worthy opponent in the lawyer for the other side: Francis Silvester himself. Silvester wanted to see how much his young student had learned in the past three years. The judge had made a special allowance so that Mat could sum up the case that another lawyer had presented.

Because the slender, red-haired young man was so short—less than five feet, six inches tall—the judge made Mat stand on a bench so that all in the courtroom could see him.

Then, with a sly smile on his lips, the judge charged the young man: "There, Mat, beat your master!"

As Mat began to speak, the courtroom fell into hushed attention. Even those who had heard him speak before were astonished at his eloquence, his confident manner, and his knowledge of the case. When the jury came back from its deliberations, it was clear that Mat had passed the test: his side had won the case.

This early victory was only the first in a series of triumphs for Martin Van Buren. Over the next 60 years, his reputation would precede him as he rose through the legal and political ranks of New York and, ultimately, the United States. By the time he became the eighth President of the United States in 1836, "Little Van" would not have to stand on a bench to command attention—his mere presence would be a signal for all to listen.

THE VAN BURENS OF KINDERHOOK

When Martin Van Buren was born on December 5, 1782, he entered the sheltered world of New York's lush Hudson River Valley. The town of Kinderhook where the Van Buren family lived was a small community. All of its residents were descendants of the first Dutch settlers who had come to New York almost two centuries before. Almost everyone in the town was related. The language that the people spoke in casual conversation was Dutch, the language of their forebears, and everyone went to church on Sundays at Kinderhook's Dutch Reformed Church.

The Van Buren family settled in Kinderhook with the first wave of Dutch immigrants in the early 1600s. By the time Martin was born, five generations of Van Burens had grown up in the community. Each had remained true to its Dutch roots, and Van Buren later boasted that there had not been "a single intermarriage with one of different extraction from the time of the arrival of the first immigrant to that of the marriage of my eldest son."

A Tavern-Keeper's Family

Martin Van Buren was the third child of Abraham and Maria Hoes Van Buren. Altogether, the Van Buren Family would eventually include nine children—the three sons and three daughters of Abraham and Maria, and two sons and a daughter from Maria Van Buren's first marriage to Johannes Van Alen, who died in the early 1770s.

It was a big family, even by Colonial standards, and Abraham Van Buren had to struggle to support it. He earned some money by growing vegetables to sell at the town's market. The bulk of his income, however, came from a tavern he owned that was a favorite meeting place for Kinderhook's gentlemen. Inside the small, cozy inn, the town's leading citizens assembled to drink and share the latest news. As in many small towns during America's early days, the tavern frequently served as a meeting hall for politicians and local officials.

Although the Van Burens were by no means wealthy, they had enough money to support themselves. They owned six slaves who worked the farmland surrounding the tavern and helped Mrs. Van Buren with the housework. Nevertheless, by Kinderhook standards, the Van Burens were poor. Among the town's residents were some of the wealthiest and most influential people in eastern New York.

Young Mat

Abraham Van Buren was not at all concerned about his social status in Kinderhook. He involved himself in his work and his family, and fulfilled his civic duties by serving as town

The house in which Martin Van Buren grew up also served as Kinderhook's most popular tavern. The Van Buren family lived on the second floor of the home, while the tavern occupied the lower floor. The Van Burens farmed the land surrounding the house. (Library of Congress.)

clerk for many years. But his young son, Martin, whom everyone called "Mat," felt deeply the sting of living on the poor side of town.

Like his brothers and sisters, Mat spent many hours working in the family tavern, where he carried firewood, swept the floor, and washed the dirty beer tankards. An intelligent and keenly observant boy, Mat listened carefully to the conversations of Kinderhook's prominent men as they discussed politics and law over their drinks. As he listened to these learned men, he dreamed of someday leaving the tavern to join them in the important and rewarding work they did. To Mat, it seemed an impossible dream. These men were educated and wealthy, and their fancy language and fine clothes contrasted sharply with his father's casual tone and rough, homespun clothing.

Kinderhook Academy

Mat Van Buren also felt the difference between his family and the town's wealthy families at the Kinderhook Academy, the local school that he attended. Although all the children in Kinderhook attended the school, many of the pupils of Mat's social standing seldom came to class because they were busy helping their parents earn a living. Many even dropped out of school after only a few years to work on family farms or in family businesses.

Mat Van Buren was one of the few students at the academy who stayed in school despite the fact that his family could never hope to have enough money to send him to college. Very early in his childhood, Mat had displayed extraordinary intelligence, and his mother was determined that he would get as good an education as possible.

The Kinderhook Academy was only a one-room wooden schoolhouse. Nevertheless, its schoolmaster, David B. Warden, was a serious teacher who carefully tutored every student who showed promise. Although smaller than most of the other boys, Mat was one of the most intelligent students in his age group, and Mr. Warden drove him to learn as much as he could.

Mat showed a great ability for language, and he quickly mastered the basics of grammar and speech. He also managed to learn the fundamental concepts of logic and the Latin language. Most important, as he himself would later note, Mat learned how to control his sometimes rash temper and his "ardent, hasty and impetuous" disposition.

READING THE LAW

The skills and knowledge that he acquired at the Kinderhook Academy would help Mat greatly in his next venture. At the age of 14, he left the academy to study law under Francis Silvester, a prominent local attorney who was also a distant relative. Although they were wealthy, the Silvester family had maintained a close and warm relationship with Abraham Van Buren. Francis Silvester was happy to be able to help his friend's bright young son pursue a profession.

His apprenticeship in Silvester's law office required Mat to leave home. As part of his arrangement with Silvester, Mat moved into the back bedroom at a dry goods store owned by Silvester's brother, Cornelius. When he was not clerking at Francis Silvester's law office, Mat swept the floor, laid the fire, and worked the counter at Cornelius Silvester's store.

Because the laws of the state of New York were so complicated and intricate, Mat devoted every free moment he had to learning them. During such moments, he would read and study the large, leather-bound law books that he borrowed from his teacher. He was such a good student that word soon spread throughout Kinderhook and the surrounding communities that young Mat Van Buren, the tavern-keeper's son, was on the way to becoming a fine lawyer.

A Budding Politician

During his apprenticeship with Francis Silvester, Mat Van Buren discovered something very interesting – law and politics were almost inseparable. Every lawyer he came into contact with, including Silvester, was deeply involved in the poitical life of the community and the state. Francis Silvester himself was a member of the Federalist Party and frequently attended party meetings and other functions.

Silvester's interest in politics spread to his young apprentice, who began to study the local political scene. What he found was that his political opinions differed greatly from those of his mentor. While Silvester's Federalist Party believed strongly in centralized government, Mat believed that the federal government should keep as much out of private life as possible. He decided that the beliefs of the Democratic-Republican Party were closer to his own views on government.

In 1800, Mat attended the district convention of Jeffersonian Republicans (another name for the Democratic-Republicans) in Troy, New York. Although he was only 17 years old, Mat impressed the politicians with his intelligence and maturity. By the time the convention ended, he had given enough persuasive speeches to enable John P. Van Ness, a fellow Kinderhook native, to be selected as the party's candidate for the U.S. Congress.

Although the Democratic-Republicans were favorably impressed with Mat, Francis Silvester was not. He and Mat had frequently argued politics between themselves, but it would not do for Silvester's apprentice to be a Democratic-Republican. Although Silvester attempted to persuade Mat to join the Federalist Party, pointing out that many of Kinderhook's leading citizens were Federalists, it was to no avail. Mat explained that he had carefully considered the views and actions of both parties and was determined to be a Democratic-Republican, just as his father, Abraham, had been before him.

For the next two years, Mat continued his apprenticeship with Silvester, enduring, he later said, "occasional tho' slight bickering between Mr. Silvester and myself" over party affiliation. By 1802, however, the two had come to an impasse. Although Mat was deeply grateful to Silvester for teaching him the law, it was clear to both of them that it was time for Mat to move on.

That same year, John P. Van Ness – the man whom Mat had helped secure the congressional nomination in 1800 – offered Mat a position in the New York City law office of his brother, William Van Ness. Mat quickly accepted, and within a few weeks was on his way to New York City.

At the age of 20, Martin Van Buren was leaving Kinderhook for the first time in his life. He was moving from a small, tight-knit community where he knew everyone into the largest city in the country. If he was nervous about the change, he did not show it. When he left Kinderhook by stagecoach for the city, he did so with an air of self-confidence and optimism that would mark his entry into the world of New York politics.

Chapter 2

Life in the Big City

When Martin Van Buren arrived in New York City, all he had with him was a small trunk of clothes, a few dollars that John Van Ness had advanced him, and a desire to learn all he could about the law. He had come to the right place. New York was the state's center of legal activity, even more so than Albany, the state capital. It was also a vital political town, where many of the most powerful men in the state—indeed, the nation—had begun their political careers. Mat Van Buren was ready to become one of those men.

CITY LIFE

On the day he arrived in New York, Mat found a small room in a boardinghouse that was within walking distance of William Van Ness' law offices. Fortunately, the room was large enough to accommodate a small desk, at which Mat could read his law books at night.

Although the rent was cheap, it was not long before Mat had spent almost all of his money. Then, after being in New York for only a few weeks, he received some rather unsettling news: William Van Ness would not be able to pay him for his work as a clerk in the law office. Mat suddenly found himself in a strange city, miles from home, with absolutely no money in his pocket.

For a few desperate days it looked as though Mat would have to return to Kinderhook. Finally, in desperation, he wrote to John Van Ness in Washington and told him that he had no money and no way of obtaining any. The congressman quickly sent off $20—a sum upon which a young man could live for weeks in 1802—and promised to send more as soon as possible.

"Temptations to Vice"

With his financial problems solved, Mat could concentrate on getting to know New York. He enjoyed walking around its wide streets—some of which, unlike the streets in Kinderhook, were actually paved—and observing the interesting variety of people who lived there. He also enjoyed the diversity of the city's social life, with its dozens of theaters, restaurants, taverns, and clubs.

John Van Ness had warned Mat that the city was a place of moral danger. "Temptations to vice are everywhere," Van Ness had written, "[and] the first and often insensible step toward it is idleness." Despite this advice, and although he had very little money to spend, Mat nevertheless sampled some of New York's social life.

After a few trips to the taverns and the clubs, however, Mat found that they were not to his liking. Although he continued to attend the theater regularly during his stay in New York, he decided to spend the bulk of his free time getting to know the city's political life.

Powerful Men

The New York political scene was very active and lively in the early years of the 19th century, and Mat Van Buren was in a perfect position to become very much a part of it. His employer, William Van Ness, was more of a politician than a lawyer, and spent much of his time engaging in political activities. Van Ness' closest political associate was Aaron Burr, who was Vice-President of the United States from 1801-1805.

Although he was serving as the nation's Vice-President, Burr, a New Yorker, still had plenty of time to exert his influence on the city's politics. When Van Buren arrived in New York, Burr was in the middle of a heated battle for control of New York's Democratic-Republican Party. Because William Van Ness was helping Burr in this struggle, his law clerk, Mat Van Buren, got an inside look at the political maneuvering.

Van Buren spent many evenings with Van Ness at Burr's lavish New York mansion. As the two older men discussed political strategies, Van Buren took mental notes. Sometimes, Burr would ask the young clerk for his opinions, and Van Buren would respond with confidence and conviction. As a result, the Vice-President took a liking to Mat and—as Van Buren himself later recalled—"treated me with much attention."

Passing the Bar

After Mat had been in New York for almost a year, the time came for him to take the New York State bar exam. Although he had been reading the law for seven years, Mat was worried about passing the exam. He had always displayed self-confidence in his dealings with much older and more ex-

Aaron Burr was Vice-President of the United States when Martin Van Buren met him in 1802. Although the two men later quarrelled over political differences, they enjoyed a warm friendship during Van Buren's stay in New York City. (Library of Congress.)

perienced men, but he was nevertheless plagued by self-doubt. He had not had much formal education, whereas most of the men he had met in New York were college educated. The majority of those who would be taking the bar exam with him were cultured young men from wealthy families.

When he was much older, Van Buren remarked that he had always regretted his lack of formal education. "How often have I felt the necessity of a regular course of reading to . . . sustain me in my conflicts with able and better educated men," he wrote in his autobiography. But Mat Van Buren had a wealth of experience to compensate for his lack of formal schooling. He had studied under two of the most noted attorneys in New York and had been present at meetings with some of the most powerful men in the country, including the Vice-President. By any standard, Mat was ready for the exam. When the results came back a few weeks after he took the test, he had passed. Martin Van Buren was now an attorney in the state of New York.

A YOUNG LAWYER

Before he could present a case before the state supreme court, Mat was required by law to complete four years of law practice. Although he had grown to like New York City, it was highly impractical for him to set up a law office there. The city was already overrun with attorneys, many of whom had better connections than he. Therefore, Mat decided that the place for him to begin to practice law was back home in Kinderhook, where his reputation already guaranteed him a substantial number of clients.

As 1803 drew to a close, Mat packed up his meager belongings and journeyed back to Kinderhook. Once there, he was offered a position in the firm of a lawyer he knew very well: James Van Alen, his half-brother by his mother's first marriage. Several years older than Mat, Van Alen had been practicing law in Kinderhook for some time. With the help of his popular and respected half-brother, Van Alen's law practice quickly boomed.

An Unpopular Decision

In early 1804, politics were on the minds of Kinderhook's men. This was an election year, one in which the United States would vote for its President and the state of New York would choose a new governor. The election was on Mat Van Buren's mind as well. He had turned 21 on the previous December 5, which meant that this year, for the first time, he was eligible to vote in an election.

In New York, the governor's post was being sought by two able men. The most notable of them was Vice-President Aaron Burr. Burr's opponent was a man named Morgan Lewis, the son-in-law of a prominent New York politician who held the position of Chief Justice of the New York State Supreme Court.

The contest was an especially bitter one because Lewis was being supported by DeWitt Clinton, the man against whom Burr had been competing for control of New York's Democratic-Republican Party. Clinton and Burr had been fierce political enemies for years, and Burr was determined to destroy Lewis as a way of striking out at Clinton.

Most of Kinderhook's leading citizens supported Burr. Many of them knew Burr personally through his association with William Van Ness, and they began campaigning throughout eastern New York on Burr's behalf. A few months before the election, the leaders of Kinderhook's Burr-for-Governor

Committee came to Mat to request his help. They wanted him to publicly declare his support for Burr.

The Burr supporters knew that Mat owed a great debt to the Van Nesses, and that Burr himself had been kind and helpful to Mat during his stay in New York City. Therefore, they expected that Mat would readily agree to work on Burr's election campaign. To their surprise, however, Mat told Burr's supporters that he could not help them in their effort. Although he did not say so publicly at the time, Mat was convinced that Lewis was the better man for the job.

Burr's supporters were shocked by Mat's refusal to help them. They quickly wrote to William Van Ness in New York to tell him that Mat was a traitor to Burr's cause. Van Ness rushed a letter to Mat, warning him to think carefully before refusing to help the Burr campaign. "I beseech you that you are not influenced by motives that will hereafter dishonor you," he wrote. Mat wrote back, saying that he felt "it would not be expedient to support [Burr]." He made it clear that despite the loyalty he felt to the Van Nesses, and despite his "strong personal prejudices" for Burr, whom he considered a friend and mentor, he could not support Burr for the governorship.

The leaders of Kinderhook soon began harassing Mat, trying to make him change his mind. They made what Mat later called "illiberal and unmanly remarks" about the young lawyer. Whenever he appeared in public, Mat was faced with a barrage of questions from Kinderhook's citizens about whom he was supporting in the governor's race.

Out of respect for the Van Nesses, who had done so much for him, Van Buren refused to publicly support Lewis. But he would not stand for the constant harassment he was getting from Burr's supporters. He reminded his attackers that "most men are not scolded out of their opinions," and vowed that he would vote for whomever he pleased on election day.

Enemies Unto Death

His refusal to support Aaron Burr in the 1804 New York governor's race got Martin Van Buren into a lot of trouble with the powerful men of Kinderhook. But within only a few months, Van Buren's instincts about Burr would be proved right, and the Van Nesses would be the first to admit it.

In July 1804, Aaron Burr challenged his long-time political enemy, Alexander Hamilton, to a duel. Hamilton was one of America's most noted statesmen and had served as the nation's first secretary of the treasury under President George Washington. He and Burr had been bitter enemies since 1800, when Burr lost his race for the presidency to Thomas Jefferson and ended up as the Vice-President. Burr believed—not altogether incorrectly—that Hamilton had caused his defeat by convincing members of Congress to choose Jefferson as President, even though Jefferson and Burr had received the same number of votes from the electoral college.

Although dueling was illegal, many men still considered it the proper way to defend their honor when they felt enemies had slandered or dishonored them. On July 11, Burr and Hamilton met in a field in Weehawken, New Jersey, and drew their pistols. After the shots were fired, Hamilton lay mortally wounded.

Burr was forced to flee the country in order to avoid being arrested for murder. Soon, word filtered through Kinderhood that another outlaw was on the loose—William Van Ness. Van Ness had served as Burr's second, or assistant, in the duel and thus was also in trouble with the law.

A few days after the incident, Martin Van Buren answered a knock on his door to find William Van Ness standing before him. Van Ness told Van Buren that he needed a lawyer, and could think of no one more qualified than his old apprentice. Although the two men had fought bitterly over the governor's race only months before, Van Buren agreed to help Van Ness in any way he could. He soon went to New York City to file the necessary legal papers. Whether Van Buren's actions had any effect is unknown, but the state eventually decided against prosecuting Van Ness for his role in Hamilton's death.

Van Ness never forgot the courage and kindness his old apprentice had shown to him in his time of need. Although Van Buren and Van Ness remained divided on political matters for the rest of their lives, they continued to enjoy a warm and intimate friendship, each grateful to the other for offering support when it was needed.

A Challenge at the Polls

When election day arrived, Mat Van Buren arose from his bed, put on his best suit, and walked to the polls. After so many years of observing the political process, he was finally able to participate in it by voting. Although he had never stated his position on the governor's race, he planned to vote for Lewis.

When he arrived at the polling place, Van Buren found Kinderhook's most powerful men assembled there. Peter Van Ness (John's and William's father) and Peter Van Schaack, one of Kinderhook's wealthiest landowners, were standing at the building's entrance. When Mat approached the table where the election officials were seated, to sign the voter's register, Van Ness and Van Schaack stepped in front of him and challenged his right to vote.

In order to vote in an election in the state of New York, one had to be a 21-year-old white male who had never been convicted of a crime and who owned an estate worth at least $200. Of course, Van Ness and Van Schaack knew that Mat was of the proper age and that he was not a felon. But they also knew, through John and William Van Ness, that Mat had very little money. Until a few months before, when he passed the bar, he had been living on John Van Ness' money. It was on this point that the two men planned to stop Mat from voting.

Once the challenge had been issued, Mat had a choice: he could decline to exercise his right to vote or he could sign a statement verifying that he was eligible on all counts to cast his ballot. Although he did not have $200, Mat knew that his half-brother and partner, James Van Alen, would put up the money if proof was required. Therefore, he signed the document stating that he was an eligible voter, then cast his ballot for Morgan Lewis.

Although Van Ness and Van Schaack were unsuccessful in stopping Mat from voting, they had accomplished their real aim: to embarrass the young man and to make it clear that they could make things hard on those who did not agree with them politically. If Mat was embarrassed, however, he did not show it. After casting his ballot, he strode out of the polling place with his head held high.

Had Aaron Burr won the governor's seat, Kinderhook's leading men could have made life very difficult for the struggling young lawyer. But Burr lost by a wide margin, and Van Buren never suffered any consequences of his first electoral decision. In fact, after the election was over, the Van Nesses resumed their warm friendship with Mat—although they all agreed not to discuss politics for a while.

Chapter 3

Lawyer and Family Man

The election of 1804 proved once again that Martin Van Buren was a maverick, a man who said and did as he pleased without regard for convention or pressure. The man who had gone against Francis Silvester to join the Democratic-Republican Party had now defied another powerful benefactor, John Van Ness, to vote for Lewis in the governor's race. It should have surprised no one, then, that Van Buren's next move would be equally controversial.

Now that he was well-known, Van Buren began receiving requests from people throughout the state who wanted him to represent them in legal actions. Many of the cases Van Buren decided to take involved a single family: the Livingstons, one of the wealthiest and most powerful families in New York.

A LAWYER FOR THE PEOPLE

The Livingstons had been well-known in New York for generations. They owned hundreds of acres of land throughout the state, much of which they rented to tenant farmers. Robert R. Livingston, the most important member of the family during Van Buren's day, had been the first chancellor of the state of New York, and the new governor, Morgan Lewis, was Robert Livingston's son-in-law.

Many New Yorkers had claims to press against the Livingstons. Some farmers lived on land that had been granted to the Livingstons by the king of England before the American Revolution. When the Livingstons tried to collect rent from the farmers, many of them sued, claiming that the Livingstons no longer held title to the land. In return, the Livingstons tried to have these farmers evicted from the land or arrested for trespassing. The result was a mountain of legal work.

Although Van Buren had helped the Livingstons politically through his support of Morgan Lewis, he did not feel he owed them any special allegiance. He knew his actions would anger the governor and his supporters, many of whom were important figures in his political party. Nevertheless, Van Buren began taking on the cases of many poor farmers who were suing or being sued by the Livingstons.

Because the Livingstons were so wealthy and powerful, they could afford to hire the best legal counsel in New York. Such notables as J. Rusten Van Rensselaer and Elisha Williams, considered by many to be two of the most gifted lawyers in the country, were hired to face Van Buren in the courtroom.

Van Buren fought these legal giants by working harder and longer than they did. He studied their courtroom styles so he could predict their strategy and exploit their weaknesses. He memorized the testimony his witnesses would give and practiced summarizing his arguments so that he would not be caught off-guard in the courtroom. He often prepared a case as though he were the lawyer for the other side, so that he could anticipate what evidence the other lawyer would introduce into court.

These strategies were so successful that Van Buren frequently won his cases. In fact, his reputation as a lawyer spread so widely that landowners began seeking his services. Although Van Buren had gained his reputation fighting against the landowners, he believed in examining each case before deciding whom he should represent. If he believed that the landowner was in the right, he would represent that side of the case.

SETTLING DOWN

By late 1806, Martin Van Buren had become one of the best-known lawyers in New York. Although he was just 24 years old, he had more cases than he could handle. As a result, he was earning a good living for the first time in his life. He began to think about settling down and starting a family of his own.

Although there were many eligible young women in Kinderhook whom Martin could consider as potential mates, one in particular caught his fancy. Her name was Hannah Hoes, a distant cousin of Martin's on his mother's side. He had known her since childhood, when they had played together at family gatherings.

Hannah was an attractive young woman with a fair complexion, curly dark hair, and a delicate, slender frame. Everyone noted how well she and Martin looked together—both of them small, slim, and light-complected. Hannah was deeply religious and very proper in her behavior, but had little formal education. One family member later described her as "a woman of sweet nature but few intellectual gifts." She and Martin began courting, and on February 21, 1807, the two were married in Catskill, New York, 25 miles outside of Kinderhook.

Hannah Hoes married Martin Van Buren in 1807. She died in 1819, long before her husband reached political prominence. Although Van Buren survived his wife by 43 years, he never remarried. (Library of Congress.)

Married Life

Hannah and Martin set up housekeeping in a small wooden house in Kinderhook. Hannah kept a clean and neat home, which was very much appreciated by her fastidious husband. Hannah and Martin's first year of marriage was made complete by the birth of a son, Abraham, in December 1807.

In early 1808, Martin decided that he would have to leave Kinderhook if he hoped to expand his law practice and broaden his political connections. He first thought of moving to New York City or to the state capital of Albany, but decided against those locations for several reasons. Both cities were glutted with lawyers, and they were large and crowded—he wanted his wife and son to live in a peaceful, country setting. After much deliberation, he decided to move to Hudson, New York, some 15 miles from Kinderhook.

Hudson was a small but busy city of 4,000 inhabitants. The city itself was about the same age as Van Buren, having been settled in 1783. It was also the seat for Columbia County, so it was the site of a lot of legal and political activity. Van Buren bought a New England-style Colonial house in which he installed his family.

Hudson Politics

No sooner had Van Buren settled into Hudson than he began exploring the local political scene. His first year in Hudson, 1808, was also an election year, and once again Van Buren was involved in the contest. He became an active supporter of Daniel D. Tompkins, the Democratic-Republican candidate for governor.

Tompkins easily won the governorship and soon afterward began to pay back his supporters. On March 20, 1808, Martin Van Buren was appointed to the post of surrogate for Columbia County.

Surrogates were judges who had jurisdiction over the probate (legal processing) of wills and the settlement of estates. What this meant for Van Buren was that he would be dealing with some of the wealthiest people in the county, gaining intimate knowledge of the amount and type of wealth they owned. It also meant that Van Buren would become better known outside of Hudson and Kinderhook, because he would be traveling throughout Columbia County dispensing justice.

On the Road

His job as surrogate did not prevent Van Buren from maintaining his law practice, and he continued to take on private cases when his other duties did not interfere. Both his legal practice and his job as surrogate kept Van Buren on the road and away from home, sometimes for weeks at a time.

Van Buren's law practice, like that of many lawyers of his day, proceeded according to an annual calendar. During the winter, he attended State Supreme Court sessions in the capital of Albany; in the spring, he journeyed to New York City to plead cases before the Court for Correction of Errors. During the summer and fall, Van Buren traveled throughout the state to courts of common pleas and courts of chancery, which were located in designated towns.

The travel was often treacherous, because in those days there were very few good roads. It was also often difficult to find a decent place to stay overnight in some of the smaller towns. Van Buren frequently slept in dirty, run-down inns and taverns, where he had to share his bed with one or two other travelers. For a man who took as much pride in neatness and cleanliness as Van Buren did, these road trips were very difficult. He was always glad to get back home to Hannah and their clean, tidy little house in Hudson. He was also glad to get home to his family, which by 1810 included a second son, John.

PUBLIC BATTLES

Van Buren's position as surrogate enhanced his already solid reputation as an important member of the Democratic-Republican Party. In 1809 he was selected to serve as chairman of Democratic-Republican meetings. The next year, Van Buren became even more active in state politics, entering into his first public political battle with one of the state's most important Federalists.

A Powerful Enemy

Van Buren had tangled with this particular Federalist before. He was J. Rustin Van Rensselaer, the lawyer who had defended the Livingston family in the cases that Van Buren took on for the farmers. During the 1810 election campaign, Van Rensselaer had said that tenant farmers were "not fit to govern themselves." This antidemocratic statement so infuriated Van Buren that he began to publicly attack Van Rensselaer. The Federalist countered with attacks against Van Buren, and before long a public feud was taking place. The two men quarrelled bitterly right up until election day, and afterward became sworn enemies.

The next year Van Buren and Van Rensselaer met again in court, where Van Buren was representing a group of citizens who were suing Van Rensselaer himself in a land dispute. The hatred between Van Buren and Van Rensselaer was so great that the trial degenerated into name calling. One of Van Rensselaer's lawyers, John Sudam, made several insulting comments about Van Buren in open court. Van Buren replied with insults of his own, and soon a shouting match was underway.

The judge in the case quickly quieted the argument, and within a few hours Van Buren had forgotten it completely.

But the next day, Van Buren received a letter from Sudam challenging him to a duel to the death.

Van Buren knew that dueling was illegal, and he had witnessed the tragedy that dueling had wrought in the Burr-Hamilton incident. Nevertheless, he accepted Sudam's challenge. He wrote back saying that he would defend his honor upon the dueling field whenever Sudam was ready. Sudam began preparing for the duel, but at the last minute his second (assistant) backed out, urging Sudam to do the same. Claiming that he could not duel without a second to assist him, Sudam called off his challenge.

Although he may have been secretly relieved, Van Buren was not about to let the incident end so abruptly. In order to make sure that everyone knew what had happened, he nailed a notice to the door of a local hotel. It explained why the duel had been canceled and called Sudam a coward.

News of Sudam's challenge and Van Buren's response quickly spread throughout New York. Newspapers around the state printed stories about the incident, a good many of them taking Van Buren's side against Sudam and the Van Rensselaers. It was better publicity than a young politician could hope for, and Van Buren took good advantage of it. Before the incident completely faded from the voter's memories, he decided to run for the state Senate.

A Hard Campaign

Before he could win the Senate seat, Van Buren first had to secure the Democratic-Republican nomination. Doing so would not be an easy task. Van Buren's old friend, William Van Ness, had decided to try his luck at the nomination, and wanted to run as a Democratic-Republican. The two men soon began to scheme against one another.

When the Democratic-Republicans met to choose a candidate, they chose Van Buren. This so angered Van Ness that he went over to the other side, supporting Federalist candidate Edward Livingston. Other angry Democratic-Republicans followed Van Ness' lead. Soon, many of the most important leaders in both political parties announced their support for Livingston. Thus deprived of the loyal party votes he had counted on, Van Buren seemed certain to lose the election.

The election was held in April 1812. Because roads were so poor and the counting so slow, it took weeks for all the votes in Van Buren's district to be gathered and counted. While the candidates waited for the results, news of partial returns reached them. By the first week in May, these returns indicated that Van Buren had lost the election.

In mid-May, Van Buren prepared to leave Hudson for New York City, where the State Supreme Court was about to begin its session. As he boarded the boat that would take him down the Hudson River to New York, Van Buren was certain that Livingston had won the Senate seat. Livingston's supporters were pretty sure themselves — several of them gathered at dockside to sneer at Van Buren as he was leaving Hudson.

After Van Buren's boat had been underway for more than an hour, however, a small rowboat came up alongside. One of the men inside the rowboat was Van Buren's brother-in-law, who reached out his hand and gave Van Buren a note. The note said that the final results of the election were in, and Martin Van Buren — not Edward Livingston — was the new state senator from the Middle District.

Chapter 4
New York Politics

The mood was grim as Martin Van Buren walked to the platform in the New York Senate Chambers to take his oath of office. The business before the Senate was so urgent that there was little time for ceremony. After a quick administration of the oath and a few handshakes, it was time for the senators to get down to business.

The crisis they faced had been building since Napoleon Bonaparte declared himself Emperor of France in 1804. Napoleon had immediately begun a series of military campaigns throughout the European mainland, and his powerful armies quickly conquered much of Europe. By 1810, Napoleon's forces were engaged in a battle with England for control of the British Isles.

The war quickly spread to the seas, where trading ships from all nations fell victim to naval assaults. The United States soon found that its ships, which were carrying trade goods to and from France, were being attacked by British naval vessels. The United States suspended trade with England in 1810 as a result of the attacks, but it did no good—American ships sailing the Atlantic continued to find themselves at risk.

These British attacks infuriated U.S. leaders in Washington, many of whom were veterans of the Revolutionary War. They were already angry with the British for supplying American Indians in the western United States with weapons. The Indians were using those weapons to attack settlers, adding more fuel to the fire. On June 18, 1812, the United States Congress declared war against England, and the War of 1812 began.

THE WAR OF 1812

Although Congress had declared a war, there was not much of a national army to fight it. During the War of 1812, the responsibility for defending territory in a particular area fell to the authorities in that region. In other words, Pennsylvania's leaders coordinated the defense of Pennsylvania, Virginia's leaders defended Virginia, and so on. In New York, the governor and the legislature had to decide how to best defend their state.

This was an important question in New York, which soon became the site of much of the fighting. New York shared a long border with Canada, an ally of Britain, and was, therefore, embroiled in some of the bloodiest and most important battles of the war.

An Avid Supporter

Van Buren had been an early supporter of war with Britain. Even before Congress had officially declared war, he was calling upon the United States to attack England, which he said had "sought to strangle us in our infancy" (a reference to the American Revolution). As soon as he took his seat in the New York legislature, Van Buren called upon the state to do all it could to help the war effort.

Because fighting the war was costly, the governors and congressmen of some states were calling for a truce with England. Several states even considered signing individual peace treaties with the British. Van Buren denounced such actions as treason. He stated his belief that each state should commit as much of its money and manpower as possible to the war.

Accordingly, he drafted a resolution called the Classification Bill. It proposed that New York draft 12,000 of its citizens—"free white males, eighteen to forty-five"—to serve in the state militia for a period of two years.

The bill was not popular with Van Buren's constituents. The farmers and businessmen he represented had no desire to leave their homes and livelihoods for two years to fight a war that the U.S. Congress had declared. Van Buren's impassioned speeches in favor of the bill won over members of the state legislature, however, and the bill passed easily. The draft soon began, and New York quickly built one of the largest and most powerful militias in the country.

New York's War Hawk

In 1814 New York was tested by one of the biggest naval battles of the war, the Battle of Lake Champlain. Up to that point, the United States appeared to be losing its fight with England. The British attacked Washington, D.C., in August, burning the Capitol Building and the White House. They then decided to attack from the north, invading New York State from Canada at Lake Champlain, in northern New York.

The Battle of Lake Champlain was fierce, but when it was over the American fleet had defeated the British. It was the last in a series of stunning naval victories for the United States. Although the victory at Lake Champlain had little to do with Van Buren's Classification Bill, it reflected well on New York. As one of the state's most vocal war leaders, Van Buren took a bit of credit for the victory. By the end of 1814, his fame as New York's toughest "war hawk" had reached Washington.

Van Buren enjoyed being trumpeted as a war leader, and he frequently referred to his role in the war. Many people, however, wondered why he had not joined the militia and defended his state from the front lines. Although Van Buren always said that he could do more as a legislator than as a soldier, he would spend years defending himself against charges of cowardice. In the 1830s, frontiersman Davy Crockett would publicly ridicule Van Buren for not fighting in the war.

The End of an Issue

In December 1814 the United States signed a peace treaty with England, ending the War of 1812. Because the treaty was signed in Europe, however, it took more than a month for news of the treaty to reach the United States. It finally arrived in February 1815.

When the peace treaty became public knowledge, Martin Van Buren suddenly found himself in an awkward position. The war was over and the United States had emerged victorious — that was good. But the war had been the major issue upon which Van Buren had built his political reputation during the previous two years. With the war over, he had no cause to trumpet, no issue to dominate.

Fortunately, Van Buren did not have to cast about for a new cause. In late February 1815, he was chosen by a state council to become New York's new attorney general. Because he was allowed to keep his Senate seat as well, Van Buren now occupied two of his state's important government positions.

A Move to the Capital

Now that he was at the center of New York politics, Van Buren decided to move his family to Albany. Wife Hannah and sons Abraham, John, and Martin, Jr. (who had been born in 1812) soon moved into a large home that Van Buren had rented in the state capital. With them came a young lawyer named Benjamin F. Butler, whom Van Buren had taken in as a law clerk in 1811 and whom the Van Burens considered to be one of the family. When Butler passed the New York bar exam Van Buren made him a full partner in his law firm.

Once he had installed his family in Albany, Van Buren could concentrate on his political career. Because he no longer had to spend time traveling back and forth between Hudson and the capital, he could more easily participate in the city's social life, most of which revolved around politics. He quickly became a fixture at Albany dinner parties, and his reputation grew.

MAKING ENEMIES

As Van Buren's fame and power grew, so did his list of enemies. He had begun amassing political enemies in 1800, when he defied the Silvesters and Kinderhook's other Federalists to join the Democratic-Republican Party. He had continued to anger fellow politicians when he went against the Van Nesses and Aaron Burr to support Morgan Lewis for the state governorship in 1804. Many observers viewed these two incidents as evidence that Van Buren put his own political advancement above loyalty to friends or to his party.

Van Buren's political maneuvering won him more enemies when he began to work on the state level. Many politicians, of course, disliked him simply because he had achieved so much power at such a young age. Others, however, claimed that they were not upset that Van Buren had risen to a position of power, but that he had used dishonest and dishonorable methods to achieve that power.

Fraudulent Voting

To back up their claims, Van Buren's enemies pointed to a number of incidents. One of these occurred in 1816, when the New York State legislature assembled for its new session. One of the legislators, a member of Van Buren's Democratic-Republican Party, was widely known to have obtained his seat through vote fraud. The first order of business for the Senate was to recall this senator and replace him with the rightfully elected candidate.

Because the Senate rolls showed 62 Democratic-Republicans to 61 Federalists, Van Buren knew that as soon as the fraudulent senator was replaced, the opposition party would have a majority. This meant that the Federalists would be able to choose the Council of Appointment, an important Senate committee that decided who would be appointed to many state offices.

If the Federalists controlled the council, Van Buren feared he would lose his appointment as attorney general. In order to prevent this, Van Buren demanded an immediate vote on members for the Council of Appointment, allowing the fraudulently elected senator to cast his ballot. As a result, the Democratic-Republicans filled the Council of Appointment with their own members, and Van Buren remained attorney general.

A Reversal on the Canal

Another incident that created enemies for Van Buren involved the Erie Canal. The state of New York had long been studying plans to build a canal that would link the Hudson River to the Great Lakes at Lake Erie. Plans for such a canal had been halted by the War of 1812. After the war ended, however, many New Yorkers renewed their support for the canal.

Martin Van Buren was skeptical. Although he agreed that the canal would help build New York's towns by bringing commerce to the state, he knew that construction would be costly. Some politicians had called for using federal funds to complete the canal. However, this was against Van Buren's belief that states should not rely on the federal government for help with internal projects.

Van Buren decided that the only way to reconcile his constituents' desire for the canal with his own instincts against it was to employ a bit of deception. He would publicly favor the canal, but privately he would delay its construction by blocking the legislation that would allow construction to begin.

This action angered Van Buren's already outspoken political enemies. They became even angrier the next year, when Van Buren suddenly tried to force legislation favoring the canal through the Senate. He thought that getting the canal bill passed would help his candidate for governor beat the incumbent, who was an enemy of Van Buren's. The maneuver was unsuccessful, however, and Van Buren's candidate lost. The only thing he gained was a growing reputation as a double-dealer.

FAMILY TRAGEDY

Van Buren's political enemies were not the only problem on his mind during his early years in Albany. A number of tragedies struck the Van Buren family in the years between 1814 and 1819. In 1814, Hannah Van Buren gave birth to their fourth son, whom Martin named Winfield Scott Van Buren (in honor of the great hero of the War of 1812, General Winfield Scott). Unfortunately, the child was sickly from birth and died after only a few weeks. The tragedy greatly affected Martin, who grieved terribly for the boy.

In 1817, Martin received another blow when his father, Abraham, died in Kinderhook. Martin's grief was lessened somewhat by the birth of a healthy son, Smith, later that year. But the following year, 1818, brought more grief when Maria Van Buren, Martin's mother, died.

Compounding these tragedies was the fact that Hannah Van Buren, Martin's wife, was extremely ill. She had been weakened by the difficult delivery of Winfield in 1814, and she grew even weaker after the birth of Smith in 1817. Although the child was healthy, Hannah was not, and the doctor confined her to bed. She grew weaker and weaker over the next two years, and in 1819 she died of tuberculosis.

In a period of five years, Martin Van Buren had lost a son, both of his parents, and his wife. The last of these tragedies was almost too much for him to bear. After Hannah's funeral in Kinderhook, Martin remained there for more than a week, unable to return to Albany even though he knew there was pressing state business to attend to. When he finally did return, circumstances there added more weight to his already heavy heart.

THE BUCKTAILS

In 1819 Martin Van Buren began to feel the effects of his years of political maneuvering. That year, New York Governor DeWitt Clinton—the man Van Buren had tried to defeat by switching his vote on the Erie Canal—decided to get even with his enemies. Using his executive privilege as governor, Clinton fired Van Buren from his post as state attorney general.

A Party War

Because Van Buren and Clinton were both members of the Democratic-Republican Party, Clinton's dismissal of Van Buren touched off a war within the party. Internal problems had

New York Governor DeWitt Clinton was Martin Van Buren's
most bitter political enemy. After Clinton fired Van Buren from
his post as New York's attorney general, Van Buren set out to
destroy Clinton's career. (Library of Congress.)

been dividing the Democratic-Republicans for many years. Now the open warfare between the party's two most powerful men caused a final split. Van Buren gathered his supporters together and formed his own faction of the party, which quickly became known as the Bucktails.

The Bucktails took their name from a tradition that Van Buren's supporters followed on patriotic holidays. Many of the Bucktails belonged to the Society of St. Tammany, a political club in New York City whose members wore deers' tails on their hats on national holidays, as a badge of their membership. Although he was not a member of the society,

Van Buren shared the political views of its members, and so his supporters soon became known as the Bucktails.

Van Buren used his influence with the Bucktails to advance his own political fortunes. He became a master at using the patronage system to his own advantage. Under the patronage system, political officials hire their supporters for important political jobs. Van Buren used patronage to get a close associate appointed to the Erie Canal Commission. Through this associate, Van Buren gained control over the Erie Canal Commission and was soon handing out canal jobs exclusively to supporters of the Bucktails.

Undermining the Governor

The major goal of the Bucktails was the political destruction of Governor Clinton. To accomplish this, the Bucktails banded together in the legislature, voting against any measure Clinton proposed. Van Buren worked behind the scenes to make sure that every Bucktail appeared on the Senate floor when a vote was about to be taken. He also tried to call votes when he knew that Clinton's supporters would not be on the floor.

These maneuvers worked to some extent, but they did not prevent Clinton from winning re-election to the governorship in 1820. That same year, Van Buren gave up his Senate post (because he had moved from Hudson to Albany, he could no longer run as a senator from the Middle District, and he decided against running for any other office). He planned to set up a law practice in New York City.

After Clinton won re-election, however, Van Buren decided to stay in Albany. From behind the scenes, he tried to undermine Clinton. Although he held no official office, Van Buren was still the leader of the Bucktails. He used his power to persuade legislators to vote against Clinton's bills and to appoint Clinton's enemies to important government posts.

The Albany Regency

Many of Van Buren's behind-the-scenes actions were successful. He soon became even more powerful than he had been
during his term in the Senate. But Van Buren was not satisfied
to remain out of the center of action. In 1821 he decided to
run for United States Senator from New York.

Van Buren had built the most powerful political organization in United States history. It later became known as the
"Albany Regency," a reference to the almost absolute power
its members wielded. Many historians point to the Albany
Regency as the first "political machine" in American politics.
With this machine behind him, Van Buren easily won his U.S.
Senate seat. In November 1821, Van Buren took his wheeling-
and-dealing brand of politics to Washington, D.C. Although
he was leaving New York, the support of the Bucktails and
the power of the Albany Regency went with him.

Chapter 5

The "Fox of Kinderhook"

The 1820s were a time of political calm in Washington. The nation's capital was in the midst of the "Era of Good Feeling," a time when party politics had been abandoned in favor of national unity. The long-standing war between the Federalists and the Democratic-Republicans was all but over; the Federalist Party itself had almost ceased to exist in the national arena. Although the Democratic-Republicans were divided into many factions, they tended to vote as a block on national issues, so for a time it seemed that party politics were dead.

Into this benevolent atmosphere stepped Martin Van Buren, the ultimate political manipulator. Van Buren had long stated his belief that "political parties are inseparable from free governments"; that is, a democracy needs a diversity of political parties to keep it democratic. In reality, however, Van Buren's viewpoint had as much to do with political survival as with democratic philosophy. He had made a career out of attacking the Federalists, and he had no intention of abandoning his central issue now that he had moved to Washington. He was determined to bring party politics back to the capital by destroying the remnants of the Federalist party

Van Buren was already well-known as a political maverick when he arrived in the nation's capital in 1821 as the newly elected U.S. senator from New York. Although his cutthroat political style made him many enemies, his elegant manners won him the affection of Washington's hostesses. (Library of Congress.)

and binding the many Democratic-Republican factions into one strong, united Democratic Party.

A WASHINGTON WELCOME

Van Buren was already well-known in Washington when he arrived there in November 1821. Everyone in town was talking about the legendary "Fox of Kinderhook," the crafty politician who had virtually controlled New York's government. His fellow statesmen could not wait to meet him, and within days of his arrival in the capital he found himself invited to a slew of parties, dinners, and dances.

Van Buren was also popular with Washington's many hostesses, the wives and daughters of famous politicians. At the age of 39, the handsome, red-haired widower was considered the most eligible bachelor in town. His erect bearing, finely tailored clothing, and elegant manners made him the focus of many young women's attention. Shortly after he arrived in Washington, he began seeing Ellen Randolf, the granddaughter of his idol, Thomas Jefferson. The two made a handsome pair at Washington's most important social events.

Getting to Work

Even before he was sworn in as Senator, Van Buren went to work. He felt he had a mission to rid the capital of the Federalists and their supporters. His first target was John W. Taylor, the Speaker of the House of Representatives and a congressman from New York. Taylor was a long-time supporter of DeWitt Clinton, Van Buren's archenemy. Van Buren talked to many Democratic-Republicans in the House, convincing them that Taylor was a Federalist at heart and was thus a threat to the Democratic-Republican Party. By the time

Congress convened for its next session, the Democratic-Republicans had removed Taylor as Speaker and Van Buren had earned another nickname—"The Little Magician."

Despite this early success, Van Buren found himself out of place once he took his Senate seat. Since 1808 he had been so involved with the politics of New York State that he had never really examined national issues. After his first few weeks as a U.S. Senator, Van Buren was utterly shaken and his old insecurity about his lack of education resurfaced in a strong form. Not only was he surrounded by the brightest and most learned men in the nation, but he was suddenly being asked to vote on national concerns, such as tariffs for international trade and regulations for the Bank of the United States—issues he had never before encountered.

Van Buren was so unnerved by his insecurity that the first time he got up to speak in the Senate chamber, he stuttered so severely that he had to sit down and compose himself before he could continue. Although he finally got through his first speech—a two-hour affair that many of the other senators feared would never end—the incident made Van Buren realize that he could never succeed in Washington until he conquered his self-doubt.

The way to gain confidence, Van Buren felt, was to learn all he could about the workings of the capital. So he began asking questions and investigating issues, refusing to offer his own opinion on a matter until he had enough information. Although this technique helped him learn, it also caused him trouble. Many people, familiar with Van Buren's reputation as a crafty politician, took his closed-mouth attitude as evidence that he was up to something.

The reputation Van Buren had gained in New York—both its good points and its bad—would follow him for the rest of his political career. Those who supported him praised his political skill, while those who oposed him claimed he was unprincipled and devious. Van Buren's first few years in Washington involved him in a series of issues that only added to this debate about his character.

The Slave Debate

In 1822 the Senate renewed its debate on an issue that had been tearing the United States apart almost since the nation's birth: slavery. The debate had split along regional lines, with the northern states calling for an end to slavery while the southern states proclaimed the economic necessity of owning slaves.

The issue facing Congress in 1822 concerned the territory of Florida, which was just being organized. Northern congressmen wanted slavery outlawed in Florida, while southern legislators wanted Florida to become a slave-owning territory. The two factions could find no middle ground.

Van Buren helped to draft a law proposing a compromise. The law restricted slaveowners from bringing new slaves into Florida, but declared that slaves already in the territory would remain in slavery. Van Buren thought that the bill, which eventually passed, would please northern congressmen who opposed the expansion of slavery as well as southerners who wanted slavery to continue.

Unfortunately, the slave bill allowed Van Buren's enemies to again claim that the New York senator was only protecting his own interests by trying to please everyone (a charge that was somewhat true, since Van Buren was trying to unite the warring northern and southern factions of his party). Van Buren's case was not helped by the fact that, technically, he himself was a slaveowner. (His slave, a man named Tom, had escaped some eight years earlier. Van Buren had made no effort to find him, however. He even told a man who volunteered to recapture Tom that he would consent to the recapture only if it could be achieved without violence.)

Presidential Politics

In 1824, as the United States prepared for another presidential election, Martin Van Buren was determined that his candidate would win the Democratic-Republican nomination. The man he supported was William Crawford, a staunch anti-Federalist and former secretary of war.

Van Buren intended to use his influence in New York to help Crawford. He would convince New York's legislature to select pro-Crawford electors for the party's nominating convention. However, because so many candidates were vying for the party's presidential nomination, Van Buren decided to try a little political maneuvering. He convinced a number of electors to vote for John Quincy Adams instead of Crawford, reasoning that if the field of candidates was thinned down to Adams and Crawford, the latter would win easily.

In the end, Van Buren outsmarted himself. The nomination indeed came down to a contest between Crawford and Adams, but a few months before the convention Crawford suffered a stroke. Most of the Crawford electors switched their votes, and John Quincy Adams became his party's candidate. A few months later, Adams was elected the sixth President of the United States. Adams later commented on Van Buren's role in the matter, saying of Van Buren, "His principles are all subordinate to his ambitions."

Another Round with Clinton

His lack of success in directing politics at the national level did not prevent Van Buren from attempting to control the New York political scene. For some time Van Buren had been working to remove his old enemy, DeWitt Clinton, from his post on the Erie Canal Commission. In 1824 he succeeded in convincing his friends among the Albany Regency to fire Clinton.

Once again, however, Van Buren's political scheming backfired. Calling Van Buren "a scroundrel of the first magnitude" and "the prince of villains," Clinton rallied hundreds of supporters to his cause. New Yorkers marched in torchlight parades to protest Van Buren's role in the Clinton case. Clinton received so much public support that he decided to run for governor, using as his platform a pledge to put an end to the Albany Regency and Van Buren's control of New York politics.

By the time election day came, there was nothing Van Buren could do to stop Clinton except vote against him. But even there, Van Buren ran into difficulty. When he reached the polls in Albany, Clinton's supporters embarrassed and angered Van Buren by doing the same thing that Burr's supporters had done in 1804: challenging his right to vote. Van Buren was forced once again to swear his oath of eligibility before he could cast his ballot. When the votes were counted, Clinton had won. For a time, at least, Van Buren's complete control of New York politics was over. Upon leaving Albany to return to the nation's capital, Van Buren called himself "as completely broken down a politician as my bitterest enemies could desire."

A MEETING WITH HIS IDOL

The one bright spot in an otherwise bleak year for Van Buren came when he was invited to the stately Monticello estate near Charlottesville, Virginia, to visit his political idol, Thomas Jefferson. The former President had heard a lot about this young man who swore allegiance to "Jeffersonian Principles," and he welcomed Van Buren warmly. For his part, Van Buren was thrilled to meet the man after whom he had patterned his political philosophy.

Van Buren later noted that he was a bit surprised at some of the political views Jefferson put forth during their meeting. Nevertheless, it was a meeting Van Buren always treasured. In Washington, the meeting between the two men set tongues wagging. It had long been rumored that Van Buren was planning to marry Ellen Randolf, Jefferson's granddaughter. Many people suspected that Van Buren had gone to Monticello to get Jefferson's blessing for the marriage. In truth, however, Van Buren never considered remarrying after his wife's death. He and Miss Randolf remained friends, but never discussed marriage.

Another Controversy

In 1826, Van Buren again found himself at the center of a controversy involving New York State. The year before, New York had opened the Erie Canal, a 363-mile, water-filled ditch that allowed barges to travel from New York City to the Great Lakes. The canal allowed cargo to travel from New York to the Midwest more efficiently than ever before, and it was a boon for the state's economy. Factories sprang up along the canal's shores, and New York City soon overtook Philadelphia as the country's largest port.

The Canal Era

The Senate debate over providing funding for canals came in 1826, at the height of what later became known as the Canal Era. During this period, canals were the most important method of transportation in the country, largely responsible for the nation's economic growth and development during the first half of the 19th century.

Canals have a history spanning thousands of years. The first recorded canals were built in ancient Egypt, China, and Babylonia, hundreds of centuries ago. Engineers in England and western Europe began constructing canals in the 12th century.

In the United States, canals were a significant transportation method as far back as Colonial times. The first canals in North America were short passages built in the 1780s: the Dismal Swamp Canal, which connected the Chesapeake Bay to Albemarle Sound; the Santee and Cooper Canal near Charleston, South Carolina; and the Middlesex Canal between Boston and the Merrimac River in northeastern Massachusetts.

Because these canals traversed such short distances, their economic impact was limited to their immediate areas. The first indication that the use of canals could affect the economy and growth of a large geographic area came in 1825, after the Erie Canal opened, connecting New York City to the western parts of New York State. The new access to goods provided by the canal had such a tremendous impact on the growth of New York that soon every state in the Union wanted to construct its own canal.

Between 1825 and 1850, scores of canal projects were undertaken throughout the country. One of the most ambitious was the Chesapeake and Ohio Canal, which attempted to link Chesapeake Bay with the Ohio River, hundreds of miles away. Another major project was the Wabash and Erie Canal, which cost so much to build that it left the state of Indiana almost bankrupt.

Around 1850 the Canal Era ended just as quickly as it had begun. The canals were replaced by a new and faster transportation system: the railroads. The first railroads in the United States were constructed between 1825 and 1830, and by 1850 it was clear that trains were far superior to the canals for transporting people and goods. The "Iron Horse," as the train was known, could move at speeds never before reached in human travel, and the laying of railroad tracks posed few of the construction problems presented by canals. Moreover, railroads could be built anywhere without having to rely on existing natural waterways.

In 1869 a coast-to-coast railroad was completed, making it possible for people and goods to travel from one side of the continent to the other—something no canal could ever do. With that, many of the nation's canals closed. Today, canals still play an important role in shipping, but they will never again enjoy the popularity they experienced during the Canal Era.

New York's success prompted the leaders of other states to consider building their own canals. The problem, however, was money. The Erie Canal had cost New York State more than $7 million to build, and many states could not afford such an expense. Soon, legislators were asking the federal government to help their states finance construction of canals.

As he had always been, Van Buren was against any federal financing of state projects. He believed that the doctrine of states' rights dictated not only that the federal government refrain from interfering in state decisions, but that the states take responsibility for their own internal construction projects. Hence, he was strongly opposed to any federal funding of state canals. Critics claimed that Van Buren was trying to prevent other states from improving their waterways so that New York, his power base, could remain one of the most powerful and prosperous states in the country. Whether or not this was true, Van Buren's stand did help him reinforce his somewhat shaky political machine in Albany.

BACK TO NEW YORK

By 1828 Martin Van Buren's political star was shining more brightly in New York than in Washington. A series of skirmishes in the Senate over a tariff bill had earned Van Buren more enemies and weakened his effectiveness as a senator. At the same time, however, he had successfully revived the Albany Regency.

Early in the year, Van Buren had persuaded the Regency to call a legislative caucus to nominate Andrew Jackson for the presidency. Jackson, a general in the War of 1812 who had earned the nickname "The Hero of New Orleans" for his successful battle against the British in that city, had built a strong alliance with Van Buren during the previous few years.

Also in 1828, the Albany Regency decided to nominate its leader for governor of New York. Although Van Buren had said a few years earlier that he had "seen enough of state politics for many years," he accepted the nomination. Throughout the summer and fall, Van Buren campaigned for the governorship while his ally, Jackson, campaigned for the presidency.

When the elections were held, both men won their fights. Andrew Jackson was elected to the presidency, and his friend, Martin Van Buren, became the governor of the country's most populous state. In the process, a new era of politics, the age of Jacksonian Democracy, was born.

Chapter 6

A Jackson Man

O n New Year's Day 1829, Martin Van Buren took the oath of office as the governor of New York. After years of unofficially controlling New York politics, Van Buren now officially held the state's highest office. It was the culmination of almost 20 years of involvement in his home state's political scene.

It was also the briefest political term Martin Van Buren ever served. A month and a half after he took up his post, Van Buren received a message from President Jackson in Washington. The new president requested that his ardent supporter come to the nation's capital to serve as secretary of state in the new administration. Van Buren didn't even have to think about it. Within a month, he had resigned the governorship, packed up his belongings, and returned to Washington.

SECRETARY VAN BUREN

Martin Van Buren seemed the perfect man for the job of secretary of state. Elegant and dignified, he knew how to deal diplomatically with the many foreign ambassadors and world leaders he met in the course of his job. Many suspected that Jackson had picked Van Buren for the post expressly because the latter had a command of social protocol. A frontiersman

*Andrew Jackson, the nation's seventh President, was Van Bu-
ren's mentor and political ally. While serving as Jackson's
secretary of state, Van Buren became the President's closest
advisor and head of the first "Kitchen Cabinet."* (Library of
Congress.)

and soldier, Jackson himself was not well-versed in society's conventions.

Van Buren became secretary of state during a period when the United States kept as much out of foreign affairs as possible. President Jackson strongly believed—as did most of his predecessors in the presidency—that the United States should keep itself free from "foreign entanglements." This policy, known as isolationism, remained a strong one well into the 20th century.

Despite the limits placed on his role, Van Buren enjoyed many accomplishments during his tenure as secretary of state. He was successful in negotiating trade agreements with the British regarding the West Indies, a group of islands in the Caribbean Sea that were rich with spices and fruits. He persuaded the government of Turkey to allow U.S. ships to sail through the Black Sea, thereby gaining access to many trading ports in Asia. He also persuaded the French government to pay the United States a large sum of money to compensate for the damage French warships had inflicted upon American ships and cargo during the Napoleonic Wars, at the beginning of the 19th century.

THE KING OF THE KITCHEN CABINET

Although his diplomatic accomplishments were notable, Van Buren's most important contribution while serving as secretary of state was as an advisor and confidante to President Jackson. Only a few months after joining Jackson's administration, Van Buren had become the leader of the "Kitchen Cabinet," a group of men who unofficially counseled President Jackson behind the scenes. The term Kitchen Cabinet, which has since been used to describe the advisors of other

Presidents, was invented by Jackson's opponents to suggest that Van Buren and other nonelected advisors were running administration policy from the White House kitchen while the real Cabinet exercised little or no power.

The Kitchen Cabinet included newspaper editors Francis Blair and Duff Green, Senator Isaac Hill of New Hampshire, noted jurist Roger B. Taney, and Jackson's nephew, Andrew Jackson Donelson. Each man was powerful and trusted by Jackson, but the undisputed leader of the Kitchen Cabinet was Martin Van Buren. Jackson trusted Van Buren implicitly, and he frequently sought Van Buren's advice on a wide range of issues that had little to do with Van Buren's appointed post in the State Department.

Jackson and Van Buren met every day to discuss the affairs of state, and soon the two became close friends. Jackson began to confide in Van Buren and frequently invited Van Buren to accompany him on his daily horseback ride. Once, as the two men rode rapidly through a wooded area, the bridle on Jackson's horse began to slip, and the President almost fell from his saddle. Van Buren quickly grabbed the bridle, preventing Jackson from falling. The President later said that Van Buren had saved his life.

Bringing Patronage to Washington

Van Buren earned the President's loyalty by protecting Jackson's interests at all costs. One of Van Buren's methods for protecting the President was to fill government posts with Jackson's supporters. As he had in New York, Van Buren used the patronage system to reward followers and punish opponents.

Many historians claim that Martin Van Buren was the first American politician to employ the patronage system on a national level. Whether or not this is true, there can be no doubt that Van Buren used patronage in a way it had never been used before. One of his first moves was to advise Jackson to fire almost every government worker who had not supported Jackson in the election. Van Buren himself carried out many of these firings, earning himself a reputation as Jackson's "hatchet man."

While many people believed that wholesale patronage was unethical, Van Buren claimed it was just good politics, and he made no apologies for his actions. Once, after he had fired an officeholder who had seemingly been doing a good job, Van Buren was asked why the man had been dismissed. "We give no reasons for our removals," Van Buren answered coldly. In fact, the reason was simply that the man's political philosophy did not match that of the President, and he was therefore considered dangerous.

As usual, Van Buren accumulated enemies as a result of his actions. One of the most relentless of these critics was John C. Calhoun, Vice-President of the United States. Calhoun resented Van Buren's growing power and his deepening friendship with President Jackson. The Vice-President had his eye on the future, when he intended to run for the presidency. Knowing that Van Buren also had presidential aspirations, Calhoun wanted to make sure that he, and not Van Buren, would have Jackson's endorsement in any future presidential contest.

In an effort to stop Van Buren's political rise, Calhoun began a smear campaign against his rival. He made sure that every unpopular decision made by the Jackson administration was attributed to Van Buren. He incited newspaper editors to write editorials against Van Buren and the Kitchen Cabinet. Before long, Van Buren and Calhoun could not be in the same room without being openly hostile to one another.

The Eaton Affair

The rift between Calhoun and Van Buren broke wide open in 1831 over what came to be known as the "Eaton Affair." The problem centered on Margaret "Peggy" Eaton, a pretty young widow who had recently married John Eaton, the secretary of war. Many people in Washington were circulating unkind rumors about Mrs. Eaton, who had once worked as a barmaid in a tavern. The stories claimed that Mrs. Eaton was a woman of loose morals, and was thus unfit to be the wife of a high-ranking Cabinet member. One particularly shocking story, which was never proved, suggested that Mrs. Eaton's first husband had actually died by suicide after learning of his wife's relationship with Secretary Eaton.

As a result of these rumors, many politicians and their wives began to snub Mrs. Eaton, refusing to recognize her in public or to invite her to social affairs. The leader of this campaign against Mrs. Eaton was Mrs. John Calhoun, the Vice-President's wife. A popular Washington hostess, Mrs. Calhoun persuaded other Washington wives to ignore Mrs. Eaton.

The rude treatment of Mrs. Eaton by Washington society made Andrew Jackson very angry. Jackson had encountered a similar problem shortly after his own marriage, when political enemies had circulated rumors about his wife, Rachel. The President was so outraged by what he deemed cruel treatment that he threatened to fire any member of his staff or Cabinet who snubbed Mrs. Eaton.

John C. Calhoun became a particular focus of Jackson's anger. Not only was Calhoun's wife leading the criticism of Mrs. Eaton, but it was widely suspected that Calhoun himself had started many of the rumors. Many people believed that Calhoun wanted to oust Secretary Eaton from his post

*Peggy Eaton, the wife of Jackson's secretary of war, was
shunned by most members of Washington society, including
Vice-President Calhoun and his wife. Van Buren's refusal to
ostracize Mrs. Eaton won him the respect and gratitude of
President Jackson.* (Library of Congress.)

and to discredit Van Buren, who was a friend and supporter of the Eatons.

By the time the rumors had circulated around the capital, Martin Van Buren and President Jackson himself were the only politicians willing to speak to Mrs. Eaton. The President respected and admired Van Buren for refusing to snub Mrs. Eaton, but others were not so gracious. Calhoun and his cronies used Van Buren's stand in the Eaton Affair to attack the secretary of state and the entire Kitchen Cabinet as not only unethical but immoral as well.

The Secretary Resigns

By the summer of 1831, criticism of Van Buren had grown so loud that it was hurting President Jackson politically. Van Buren felt that it was his duty to offer the President his resignation. At first, President Jackson refused the resignation, saying that he would under no circumstances allow his critics to deprive him of a trusted advisor. Eventually, however, the President realized that the only way to quiet his critics was for Van Buren to resign.

Before Van Buren could resign, however, President Jackson made him agree to a deal. The President would accept Van Buren's resignation only if Van Buren would accept an appointment as minister to Great Britain and then agree to be Jackson's vice-presidential running mate in the 1832 election. Van Buren eagerly agreed, as the deal allowed him to advance his political career as well as knock his rival, John C. Calhoun, from the Democratic ticket.

Van Buren resigned in the early fall of 1831. Secretary of War Eaton turned in his resignation on the same day. President Jackson then fired all of Calhoun's supporters in the Cabinet. Although he could not fire Calhoun (an elected Vice-President can be removed only by Congress or through resignation), Jackson made it clear to Calhoun that he now considered his Vice-President neither a friend nor a political ally.

THE CONFIRMATION BATTLE

Martin Van Buren spent Christmas of 1831 in London. He had arrived there about a month earlier with his son, John (now 21 years old), and the author Washington Irving, a close friend. Van Buren rented a fashionable house on Statford Place, where the three men settled in to enjoy the holidays.

Van Buren was glad to be spending time with one of his children. Ever since Hannah's death 12 years earlier, his four sons had been living with relatives, and he did not have much opportunity to get to know them. Although he visited his sons whenever he could, Van Buren did not begin to spend long periods of time with them until after they became adults. Once they were grown, however, Van Buren's sons accompanied him as often as possible.

Bad News from Washington

Van Buren had just settled into his new home in London and was about to get down to work when he received some disturbing news from Washington: Congress was questioning his appointment to the minister's post. President Jackson had appointed Van Buren as minister while Congress was in recess. When the legislature opened its new session in January, the appointment came up for confirmation by the Senate.

There was nothing unusual in the fact that the Senate was debating Van Buren's appointment; the Senate must confirm many nominations made by the President. What worried Van Buren were the rumors that many Senators planned to vote against him.

The leader of this anti-Van Buren movement was John C. Calhoun. As Vice-President, one of Calhoun's functions was to preside over the Senate. Although the Senate president has limited voting power (he may vote only to break a tie), he has considerable power to influence Senate members. Calhoun was an expert at wielding this power, and in January 1832 he decided to use it against Martin Van Buren.

Serious Charges

At the confirmation hearings, Calhoun and his supporters attacked Van Buren mercilessly. They claimed that Van Buren had purposely driven a wedge between President Jackson and Calhoun in order to enhance his own standing with the President. They also said that Van Buren had convinced some Cabinet members to quit, and had persuaded Jackson to fire others, simply to advance his own career. Further, they accused Van Buren of firing officeholders for no reason, and of granting federal jobs to his supporters "to the exclusion of almost all others."

These charges were damaging, and, unfortunately for Van Buren, they were largely true. Self-advancement had been Van Buren's primary motive in the Eaton Affair and the events that followed, and he had used patronage to reward his followers and punish his detractors. The fact that Van Buren was sincerely loyal to President Jackson and that he believed that his actions were not unethical, but merely politically astute, made little difference to his attackers.

"It Will Kill Him, Sir"

Van Buren's supporters in the Senate quickly came to his defense. They charged that the debate amounted to nothing more than a vendetta against Van Buren by Calhoun. Indeed, the

John C. Calhoun resented Van Buren's close relationship with President Jackson and made several attempts to destroy Van Buren's career. Ultimately, however, it was Calhoun's political career that suffered when Jackson chose Van Buren as his vice-presidential running mate in the election of 1832. (Library of Congress.)

confirmation hearings degenerated into a name-calling session, with little discussion about Van Buren's qualifications for the minister's post.

The debate split the Senate right down the middle, and when a vote was taken the result was a tie. Unfortunately for Van Buren, the man who would now cast the deciding vote was Calhoun, the Senate president. Naturally, Calhoun voted against his enemy, defeating Van Buren's nomination as minister to Great Britain.

Calhoun was jubilant at Van Buren's defeat, gleefully telling a friend, "It will kill him, Sir, kill him dead!" But others were not so sure. Many senators told Calhoun that he had been careless in making an enemy out of such a wily and resilient political animal as Van Buren. Senator Thomas Hart Benton of Missouri told Calhoun, "You have broken a minister, and elected a Vice-President."

THE JACKSON TICKET

Within a few months, Senator Benton's prophecy would come true. When the Democratic-Republicans met for their national convention in the spring of 1832 — the first national nominating convention in American history — they nominated Andrew Jackson as their presidential candidate, as the party had done in 1828. But they nominated Martin Van Buren, not John C. Calhoun, as their vice-presidential candidate. Later that year, the Jackson-Van Buren ticket swept to victory at the polls, and Martin Van Buren became the new Vice-President of the United States.

Van Buren occupied a vice-presidency vastly different from that of his predecessor, Calhoun. Whereas Calhoun's split with Jackson had resulted in Calhoun concentrating his power in the Senate, Van Buren worked closely with the President on matters concerning the executive branch of government. Jackson, who was very ill during his last term, trusted Van Buren to handle matters as he himself would, and frequently allowed the Vice-President to act in his stead when he was too ill to attend a meeting.

The Great Bank Debate

Because of Jackson's illness, Van Buren became involved in the most sensitive issues facing the presidency. And no issue was more sensitive than that of renewing the charter of the Bank of the United States. This controversial subject would occupy most of Van Buren's time during his tenure as Vice-President.

The Bank of the United States was a privately owned financial institution that had a charter from the U.S. government to hold government assets and conduct the government's financial business. Although the bank had handled the government's money well, President Jackson felt that it was wrong for a privately owned bank to have so much control over the national treasury. He believed that this gave the bank's stockholders too much power over the country's economy.

The bank's federal charter was due to be renewed in 1836. However, in 1833 President Jackson decided to begin attempts to defeat renewal of the charter. A few senators then tried to thwart Jackson by rushing a bill to recharter the bank through Congress. The bill passed, but when it reached President Jackson for his signature, he vetoed it.

The President and his advisors then asked Vice-President Van Buren to choose a number of so-called "pet banks" to hold the government's assets. Van Buren, however, doubted that this plan would be effective. Furthermore, he feared that choosing the pet banks himself would be a dangerous political move, since any problems resulting from the scheme would probably be blamed on him. Therefore, Van Buren refused to select the pet banks, although he continued to support the President's stand against the Bank of the United States.

Van Buren may have made a mistake in allowing others to choose the pet banks. Many of the banks that were eventually selected invested government funds unwisely, causing trouble for the nation's economy. But even though he had steered clear of involving himself directly in the issue, Van Buren still received much of the criticism for the decision.

By 1836, the bank issue had caused such hard feelings in Washington that Martin Van Buren was receiving death threats. During the last year of his vice-presidency, Van Buren carried two pistols with him whenever he appeared in public. The pistols were hidden under his coat, where he could easily reach them if trouble arose.

THE RUN FOR THE PRESIDENCY

Although the bank issue had made the President and his Vice-President rather unpopular among some of the people in Washington, most Americans still loved their President. In fact, Jackson was one of the most popular Presidents of all time. Most American citizens respected him because he was a frontiersman from Tennessee rather than a well-educated easterner. They saw his actions regarding the Bank of the United States as one more example of Jackson's efforts to protect the common man, instead of allowing a few rich people to control the country.

This good feeling about Jackson also extended to his Vice-President, even though Van Buren was more like the easterners Jackson fought against than the pioneers who identified with the President. Van Buren had won President Jackson's trust and respect, and that was good enough for many people. In 1836 Van Buren decided to take advantage of this trust and respect by running for the presidency. President Jackson immediately announced his support for Van Buren.

"A Tissue of Intrigues"

Now that Van Buren was running for the nation's highest office, the many enemies he had accumulated over the years came out in force. Some of the most noted politicians in the country began to attack the candidate, and their attacks were vicious and personal. For example, Senator William Seward of New York called Van Buren "a crawling reptile," and urged his constituents to vote against him.

Another of Van Buren's attackers was Davy Crockett, the frontiersman and congressman who had previously criticized Van Buren for not fighting in the War of 1812. Crockett attacked Van Buren in print by writing a mock biography of the candidate. The book claimed that Van Buren's entire political career was nothing more than a "tissue of intrigues" laid for the sole purpose of gaining the presidency. (A few months after the book's release, Crockett was killed while fighting the Battle of the Alamo. Unwilling to launch a counterattack against a dead hero, Van Buren refused to respond to the charges made in Crockett's book.)

Hatred of Van Buren was so strong in some quarters that some members of his own party broke off to form the "No-Party Party," the goal of which was to stop Van Buren from gaining the Democratic-Republican nomination. The group's name itself was an attack against Van Buren, who insisted that party politics was the keystone of a democracy. The No-Party group joined in the attacks upon Van Buren's character and career. Despite their efforts, however, Van Buren easily won the Democratic-Republican nomination.

A Dirty Campaign

The presidential campaign of 1836 was a very dirty one. Both Van Buren and his opponent, William Henry Harrison, concentrated less on the issues than on attacking one another. Harrison's camp called Van Buren "the mistletoe politician, nourished by the sap of the hickory tree." This was a reference to Jackson's nickname, "Old Hickory," suggesting that Van Buren, like the mistletoe plant, was a parasite that could live only when attached to a strong host.

Van Buren was indeed a "mistletoe" candidate in the election of 1836. The election marked the first time in American history that a U.S. President actively campaigned for his successor. Most historians agree that Van Buren probably would not have been elected the eighth President of the United States had not Jackson supported him so vigorously. With his election to the presidency in 1836, Van Buren became the last sitting Vice-President to be elected President until November 1988, when Vice-President George Bush was elected the 41st President of the United States.

Chapter 7

The "Little Magician" in the White House

O n the first Saturday in March 1837, a stately horse-drawn carriage pulled up in front of the Capitol Building in Washington, D.C. The two people inside the vehicle were the most famous men in the country. One was the tall, gaunt, aging man who was vacating the presidency; the other, the short, plump, middle-aged man who was taking his place. The carriage itself was famous, having been made of wood taken from the American frigate *Constitution*, the legendary Revolutionary War naval vessel more commonly known as "Old Ironsides."

The crowd assembled outside the Capitol Building cheered as Andrew Jackson and Martin Van Buren stepped from the carriage. Everyone suspected that this would be Jackson's last public appearance. He was so ill that Van Buren even offered to let him stay on in the White House until he was strong enough to travel back to his home in Tennessee. The large crowds that gathered in Washington's streets were more eager to see Jackson, the out-going president, than Van Buren, their new leader.

Van Buren was still riding high on Jackson's popularity when he took the presidential oath of office on March 4, 1837. Shortly afterward, however, the Panic of 1837 caused the new President's popularity to plummet. (Library of Congress.)

The new President did not enjoy the same warmth and affection from the people that his predecessor had. Rather, it was his loyalty to Andrew Jackson that had elected Martin Van Buren to the presidency. Little did he know that on his inauguration day—the day that he took a backseat to Andrew Jackson—he was enjoying the greatest popularity he would know during his presidency. The next four years would mark a continual decline in Martin Van Buren's political fortunes. By the time he left office in 1841, the "Little Magician" had lost all his political power.

INAUGURAL PROMISES, ECONOMIC REALITIES

When Martin Van Buren stepped up to the platform that March morning, he took his oath of office alone. No Vice-President was sworn in with him that day, because no vice-presidential candidate had received enough electoral votes to claim the office (in Van Buren's day, the President and Vice-President were elected separately, rather than as a unified ticket). Van Buren's choice for Vice-President, Richard M. Johnson, would be sworn in later in the year, after the Senate voted him into office.

Van Buren's inaugural address was a fairly typical one, full of promises and reassurances. He discussed the slavery issue, refusing—as he always had—to side with either the northern abolitionists or the southern slaveholders, instead urging "calm and enlightened judgement" in dealing with the problem. He also addressed the nation's economy, promising his constituents that the country's finances were "perfectly secured."

The Panic of 1837

Even as he delivered his inaugural address, Martin Van Buren knew that the nation's economy was not "secured." A month earlier, violent riots had swept New York City when merchants attempted to raise the price of flour from $8 to $15 per barrel. Angry political activists had broken into a warehouse and dumped flour into the streets, where hundreds of hungry New Yorkers shoveled it into bags and boxes to take home. For many of the people in the crowd, the flour would be used to make the first bread they had eaten in days. Poor financial conditions in the city had already cost many people their jobs.

By mid-April, just a few weeks after Van Buren's inauguration, brokerage houses (companies that trade in stocks and bonds) began to close. By mid-May, many banks shut down, unable to pay their customers the money they wanted to withdraw. The failure of the banks caused financial problems for industries as well, and soon factories throughout the Northeast were closing. The closing of the factories, in turn, led to people losing their jobs. Soon, jobless people who could not pay the rent on their homes and apartments were being evicted, causing housing operated by charity organizations to be overrun with penniless families.

The economic crisis quickly spread to the southern United States. Cotton planters lost millions of dollars when northern textile mills closed down, thus depriving them of a market for their product. Soon, southerners were packing up their belongings and heading west in search of better times. This mass migration further strained the economy, as merchants lost their customers.

By early June, the entire country was in the grips of the worst economic depression since winning its independence. The depression soon became known as the "Panic of 1837." Panic is exactly what it caused. An Englishman who was visiting America at the time remarked, "The conquest of the land by a foreign power could hardly have produced a more general sense of humiliation and grief." The principal focus of this humiliation and grief was Martin Van Buren, who was now charged with finding a solution to the nation's economic problems.

Jackson's Legacy, Van Buren's Problem

Before he could solve the country's financial woes, Van Buren had first to examine their cause. The economic problems that led to the Panic of 1837 had been slowly building during the Jackson administration. During the early years of Jackson's presidency, America's western frontier had been opened for settlement. Thousands of easterners thereupon headed west to stake land claims. However, many of these people bought their land on speculation—that is, they bought land on credit, without the money to back up their purchases.

In an effort to stop land speculation, which he felt could lead to financial disaster, Jackson issued an order (called the specie circular), which demanded that all land purchases in the West be made with hard currency—that is, gold and silver coins. The result of Jackson's order was that millions of dollars in gold and silver were shipped west. Soon, banks in the East had no hard currency with which to pay their debts.

Banks now began to offer paper credits (documents, signed by a bank official, that represented hard currency) to their customers in place of hard currency. The public placed little faith in these paper credits, however, and with no hard money to back them up, the paper credits quickly became worthless. This caused a "run" on the banks, in which people demanded that they be permitted to withdraw all their funds in hard currency. Unable to meet these demands, the banks closed down.

Another reason for the failure of the banks was that wealthy financiers had been manipulating the economy for their own benefit. Nicholas Biddle, for example, the owner of the Bank of the United States, had been sending millions of dollars in hard currency to England, where he could get higher interest than he could in the United States. This added to the drain of hard currency. Furthermore, Biddle and other bankers had been manipulating stocks, buying and selling blocks of stock with the sole intention of driving up the prices of certain stocks while lowering the prices of others. Although Biddle and his cohorts had profited, many other individuals and businesses had lost large sums of money.

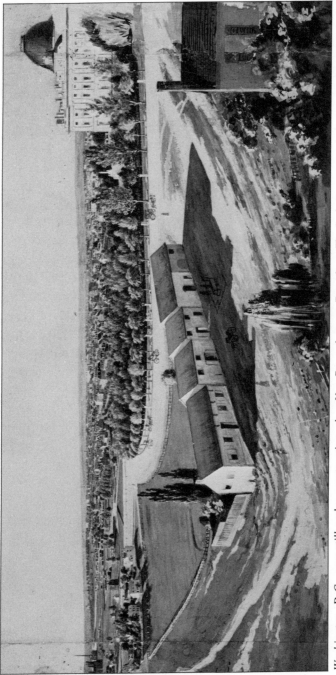

Washington, D.C., was still under construction when Van Buren became President. The lack of federal funds caused by the Panic of 1837 brought construction to a halt in the capital and throughout the country. (Library of Congress.)

The financial panic had also been caused by the actions of American merchants, who were suffering under a huge trade deficit. The merchants had been importing more items from foreign countries, most notably England, than they had been exporting. As a result, more money was leaving the country than was coming in. Soon, the merchants were in debt to the foreign countries, and with all the hard currency gone, they could not pay their debts.

These monumental financial problems affected every sector of American society, including the government. Like most of the banks in the country, the majority of the pet banks that held the nation's assets failed, and the national treasury was soon bankrupt. The country had no money to pay its bills — no money to buy arms and military equipment, to undertake construction, to fund social programs, or to pay its workers.

Many people, both in and out of government, placed the blame for this crisis squarely on Martin Van Buren. After all, he had been Jackson's right-hand man. If Jackson's policies were at fault, then Van Buren would have to accept the responsibility. Despite his efforts while Vice-President to avoid being associated with the pet banks scheme, Van Buren found himself bearing the brunt of the blame.

Formulating a Plan

Business and political leaders around the country demanded that Van Buren call a special session of Congress to deal with the Panic of 1837. (In a special session, Congress enacts legislation aimed at one specific issue or problem.) Van Buren agreed that a special session was needed, but he was reluctant to call one before he had time to formulate his own plan for dealing with the Panic. Although it angered many people, Van Buren delayed calling a special session until September. Meanwhile, he drafted his own measures for solving the country's financial crisis.

Van Buren's solutions for the problem were based on his basic political philosophy. The President did not believe that the federal government was responsible for the financial fortunes of individual citizens. For this reason, he felt no strong obligation to create programs to aid those people who had lost their jobs or homes as a result of the Panic. He also did not believe that the government had the right or the duty to interfere in the affairs of private industry. Hence, he did not aim his efforts at helping individual businessmen improve their businesses. Rather, Van Buren believed that his sole financial obligation as President was to restore to the federal treasury the funds it had lost as a result of the Panic.

Van Buren concluded that the only way to ensure the security of federal funds was to create an independent treasury to hold all national assets. Unlike the Bank of the United States or the pet banks that had previously held federal monies, an independent treasury would hold only federal funds. Thus, it would be immune to bank closures or to "runs" on banks. Van Buren proposed that the government gradually withdraw its funds from the pet banks and deposit it in small "subtreasuries" throughout the country, where it would be overseen by government officials.

An independent national treasury is such an integral part of the United States' current financial system that it is hard to understand just how radical an idea it was during Van Buren's time. Many politicians and businessmen, however, felt that creating an independent treasury would lead to the very destruction of democracy. "Is it right to *isolate* the government from the general interests & wants of the community?" asked Virginia Senator William C. Rives. Rives believed that withdrawing government funds from state banks would lessen the President's "powerful & salutary influence on the condition of the general currency."

Van Buren's traditional enemies painted the plan as one

more attempt by the President to "extend executive patronage and power" beyond its traditional limits. They believed that Van Buren wanted to create more federal jobs for his friends while he gained more personal control over the federal coffers. In the end, the issue boiled down to a debate over the causes of the Panic. As Connecticut Senator John M. Niles, a supporter of Van Buren's independent treasury, remarked, "Our opponents charge the difficulties [of the current banking system] . . . to the government; we charge them to the Banks. This is the issue between us."

The Role of the Newspapers

Some of the loudest voices in the debate over Van Buren's independent treasury proposal came from the nation's newspapers. Just as they do today, newspapers during Van Buren's time played an important role in the public debate over government policy. However, unlike modern newspapers, the newspapers in Van Buren's day did not attempt to report objectively. Rather, the owners and editors of newspapers worked together with politicians to present a particular side of a story. Newspapers were known for their political affiliations, and some even had such names as *The Republican* or *The Democrat*.

Politicians sought out newspapers to represent their views, often feeding editors stories about the opposition. Van Buren himself was a master of the newspaper game. When he was leading the Albany Regency in New York, Van Buren had almost absolute control of the content of the Albany *Argus*, a paper sympathetic to Regency interests. During his presidency, he used the Washington *Globe* to express his views.

The President could not control all of the nation's newspapers, however. When the Panic hit, opposition

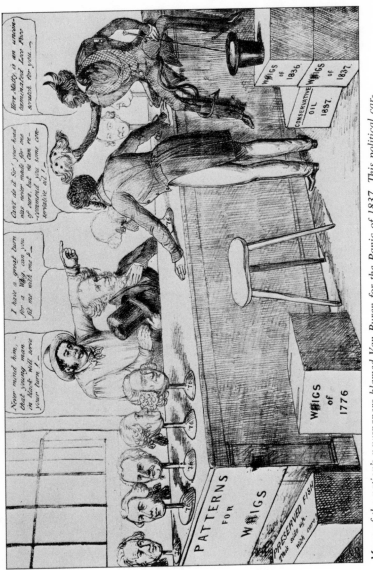

Many of the nation's newspapers blamed Van Buren for the Panic of 1837. This political cartoon depicts Van Buren (seated) as attempting to disguise himself as a Whig to avoid blame for the Democrats' alleged mishandling of the U.S. Treasury. (Library of Congress.)

newspapers went on the warpath against him. Throughout the summer of 1837, Van Buren and his policies were attacked in newspapers throughout the country. Surprisingly, the attack was led by the Albany *Argus*. Angered by Van Buren's stand on an independent national treasury, the editors at the *Argus* abandoned the President, even refusing to print his administration's views on the causes of and solutions to the Panic.

Other newspapers soon joined in. Thomas Ritchie, the editor of a newspaper in Virginia, believed that an independent treasury would completely "jar the social system," and he used his paper to argue vehemently against it. Many newspapers attacked not only the treasury plan but Van Buren himself. The New York *Herald* said that Van Buren "began life by trundling cabbages to market in Kinderhook," and was thus incapable of finding a solution to a problem as complicated as the Panic. Further, the paper claimed that "Martin Van Buren and his atrocious associates" were solely responsible for causing the country's financial problems. By the end of the summer, Van Buren's image—and that of his independent treasury plan—was badly tarnished.

The Panic Session

In September 1837 the United States Congress assembled for the Panic Session, a special session convened to draft legislation for solving the nation's financial crisis. Van Buren himself had set the date for the session, believing that by the fall of 1837 his independent treasury plan would have won broad approval. Ironically, the result of the delay had been to give Van Buren's opponents time to think of their rebuttals to his plan.

Although all the legislators truly wanted to solve the nation's problems, the Panic Session quickly degenerated into one of name-calling. The Whigs, a political party that had

82   *Martin Van Buren*

Moments of Hope During the Panic

While Martin Van Buren was trying desperately to salvage the national economy after the Panic of 1837, many talented U.S. citizens were working to improve other aspects of American life. The following are some of the most notable events that occurred during Van Buren's term:

- Ralph Waldo Emerson delivered his famous "American Scholar" address, calling for greater academic freedom and liberation from European ideas.
- The American Peace Society, the nation's first active peace organization, was formed.
- Horace Mann was named secretary of the Massachusetts Board of Education, the country's first public school board.
- Edward Hoyle wrote his famous book on the rules of card-playing, which remained the country's standard game manual for generations.
- Mount Holyoke Female Seminary, the country's first college for women, was founded by Mary Lyon.
- The United States Patent Office issued the first patent on rubber to inventor Charles Goodyear.
- Explorer Charles Wilkes embarked on a four-year voyage through the Pacific and Antarctic Oceans to gather scientific information.
- The Underground Railroad, a chain of safehouses designed to help southern slaves escape to the North, was organized.

- Erastus B. Bigelow developed a power loom capable of weaving two-ply carpets, revolutionizing the carpet-making industry.
- Abner Doubleday of Cooperstown, New York, created the rules for the game of baseball.
- William F. Harnden began the nation's first express package delivery service, transporting goods between Boston and New York via the railroads.
- D.S. Rockwell invented a horse-drawn corn planter that could plant two rows of corn at the same time, an invention that greatly aided American farmers.
- The country's first dental school, the Baltimore College of Dental Surgery, was incorporated.

recently gained a lot of power, attacked the Democrats and Van Buren's plan for an independent treasury. Henry Clay, the famous Whig senator from Kentucky, said, "It was paper money that carried us through the Revolution, established our liberties, and made us a free and independent people." Van Buren, he charged, was "cold and heartless," and did not care that the American public was "a bleeding people." He blamed Jackson's and Van Buren's policies for the Panic, saying that "a hard money Government and a paper money people" had caused the crash.

Van Buren's supporters launched counter charges, but they were to little avail. In the end, Van Buren's Subtreasury Bill narrowly passed the Senate but lost in the House. Other Van Buren measures lost as well. His plan to raise revenues by selling some federal property to farmers at inexpensive prices was voted down in both houses of Congress.

However, Van Buren did succeed in getting some measures passed during the Panic Session. The first of these allowed the government to issue $10 million in interest-bearing notes as payment of the government's current debts. Another granted importers the right to pay customs dues (taxes on goods brought into the country from other nations) in paper money, rather than hard currency. This made it possible for American importers and exporters to help the economy by increasing their overseas trade.

An Angry Public

The measures passed during the Panic Session helped somewhat to ease the nation's economic crisis, but it would be many months before the economy improved dramatically. Meanwhile Martin Van Buren's popularity with Congress, the press, and the people continued to decline. On November 22, 1837, an angry mob marched on the White House, firing a heavy cannon and screaming insults at the President.

Also in November, elections held around the country served to denounce Van Buren's administration. In almost every state, the Whigs soundly defeated Van Buren's party (now known simply as the Democratic Party). In Albany, members of the Regency turned against their former leader, and Van Buren suffered the humiliation of seeing his party lose in his home state.

FOREIGN POLICY AND THREATS OF WAR

In December 1837 Van Buren's attention was diverted from the country's economy by a problem to the north. A group of Canadians had rebelled against the British rulers of Canada, demanding independence. The rebels had gotten many of their ideas about independence from their neighbors in the United States, who had won a similar battle for independence less than 60 years before.

The Canadians had no trouble finding support for their actions among the people of the United States. Americans still clearly remembered their own struggle for independence from the British. Moreover, anti-British sentiment, fueled more recently by the War of 1812, still ran high. Because of this, the rebel Canadian leaders began recruiting soldiers from among their American neighbors.

Because Canada shares a long border with New York State, many New Yorkers became involved in the rebellion. Rensselaer Van Rensselaer, a member of one of New York's most prominent families, became the leader of the revolt, taking the title of Commander of the Patriot Army. On December 15 Van Rensselaer led an assault on Navy Island in the Niagara River, on the border between New York and Canada. Within days, more than 800 soldiers, many of them Americans, had joined Van Rensselaer and his Patriot Army on Navy Island. The soldiers planned to launch an attack on the Canadian mainland from the island.

The Attack on the *Caroline*

Before the Patriot Army could launch its attack, British forces began to shell Navy Island with cannon fire. Then, on December 29, a group of British and loyal Canadian troops attacked the American steamship *Caroline*, which had been carrying troops and ammunition to the Patriot Army. The British killed one of the ship's American passengers and threw his body overboard. The next morning, people living along the river saw the bloody body floating in the water.

When news of the attack on the *Caroline* spread, people throughout New York demanded revenge. They expected

This portrait of Van Buren, by Daniel Huntington, was painted during his term as President. Van Buren's serene expression belies his difficult presidency, which saw a financial crash, a war with the Indians, and several border skirmishes with Canada and Mexico. (Library of Congress.)

the United States Army to enter the conflict and begin a war with the British. Officials in Washington, however, had no idea that Americans were at war with British soldiers. News traveled so slowly in those days that it was not until January 6, 1838, that President Van Buren learned of the attack. Meanwhile, people in New York grew angrier.

When Van Buren found out about the *Caroline* attack, he too was angered by the British action. But he also was angered by the actions of those Americans who had decided to wage war on a foreign country without consulting Washington—such an action was a crime. Furthermore, the policy of Van Buren's administration was one of reconciliation with Britain, which was one of the United States' major trading partners and thus important in helping the country solve its financial problems. The last thing Van Buren wanted was another war with the British.

On January 8 Van Buren sent Congress a special message regarding the attack on the *Caroline*. He asked Congress to station soldiers along the border between New York and Canada to prevent further violence. Van Buren saw to it that his old friend, General Winfield Scott, was put in charge of the troops.

General Scott immediately marched his army to the Canadian border, where he instructed the Patriot Army on Navy Island to lay down its weapons and disband. Then, on orders from President Van Buren, he arrested Rensselaer Van Rensselaer and charged him with the crime of accepting a military post from a foreign government (Van Rensselaer was eventually convicted and imprisoned for this crime). A few skirmishes broke out in the following months, including a reprisal for the *Caroline* incident in which a group of Americans burned the Canadian steamship *Sir Robert Peel*. However, for all intents and purposes, the rebellion ended with Van Rensselaer's arrest.

The Republic of Texas

As 1838 progressed, Van Buren again faced problems on one of the country's foreign borders—this time, on the border with Mexico. The problem had begun years before, when American settlers in the territory of Texas had decided to fight for independence from Mexico, which at that time controlled the area. In 1836, after the Battle of San Jacinto, the settlers won their independence and declared Texas an independent Republic.

The leaders of the Republic of Texas then wanted the United States to recognize Texas as a sovereign nation. President Jackson was reluctant to grant recognition, however, because he did not want to create hostility between the United States and its defeated neighbor, Mexico. Jackson decided that the responsibility for recognizing Texas should be up to Congress, claiming that Congress alone must decide how to handle such a risky situation.

Congress debated the issue for months, finally deciding to recognize the independent Republic of Texas on March 1, 1838, three days before Van Buren's inauguration. But recognition of their republic was not what the Texans really wanted from the United States. Once the United States had officially recognized their independence from Mexico, the Texans wanted the American government to annex Texas (that is, make it part of the United States).

President Van Buren was strongly against making Texas a state or a territory of the United States. He knew that annexation would result in a debate over whether Texas should be a slaveholding state or a free state. Van Buren had learned during the debate over Florida, when he was in the Senate, that the slavery issue could only hurt him politically. Therefore, he continued to oppose annexation of Texas throughout his presidency. Not until 1845, when Van Buren was no longer President, was Texas admitted to the Union.

The Aroostook War

In 1839 another conflict arose between the United States and England, this time on the border between Maine and the Canadian province of New Brunswick. This conflict involved disputed territory along the Aroostook River, which runs through Maine and into Canada. The United States and England had been fighting over the land since 1783, when both nations claimed logging rights to the area.

In 1831 both countries appealed to an impartial party for a solution to the problem, and the king of the Netherlands proposed a compromise. However, the United States refused to accept the solution, believing that it favored the British.

In January 1839 the governor of Maine asked his state legislature to send troops to the Aroostook region to protect the right of American citizens to log in the area. A month later, Canadian officials arrested Rufus McIntire, an American land agent who was trying to secure logging rights for Americans. Furious, the governor of Maine mobilized his militia and prepared for war.

The territory of New Brunswick in Canada also mobilized its militia, thus beginning what became known as the Aroostook War. Although no one fired a shot, tensions were high, and President Van Buren feared there would again be bloodshed between the British and the Americans. The U.S. Congress also expected warfare and even authorized the expenditure of $10 million to fight the Aroostook War.

The money was never spent, however, because the Aroostook War never materialized. President Van Buren again called on his friend, General Winfield Scott, to mediate a solution. Scott went to the area and arranged a truce while Van Buren's administration worked with the British to establish a boundary commission to settle the dispute. Once again, Van Buren had avoided war.

The Indian War

One of the reasons Van Buren was so careful about involving the United States in any wars with its neighbors was that the country was already at war. In Florida, troops of the United States Army were fighting with American Indians who refused to give up their traditional tribal lands to white settlers.

The United States had long had a policy of obtaining land where white people wanted to settle by moving American Indians to lands west of the Mississippi River. Officially, the government's policy was to "encourage" the Indians to move west. In reality, this "encouragement" was carried out by the Army, which forced the Indians to move off their lands and imprisoned or killed those who refused.

While some Indian tribes had traditions of nonviolence that prevented them from fighting the Army, others did not. In Florida, the Seminole Indians had launched a war against the first white settlers, and they continued their assault when the Army arrived to support the settlers in 1835. About 2,000 Seminoles fought a guerilla war against the settlers and the Army troops who had been sent to help them.

Van Buren had always supported plans to move the Indians west; indeed, he provided more than $16 million for such moves during his term. He also allotted several million dollars more to help the Army fight the Seminoles, an act that weakened his popularity even further. The costly and bloody war against the Seminoles was extremely unpopular in the North, where those affected by the Panic of 1837 could not understand how the President could spend millions fighting the Indians in Florida while American citizens were starving. As the Indian War dragged on, Van Buren's popularity continued to decline.

THE VAN BUREN WHITE HOUSE

Despite the chaos that surrounded Van Buren during his term, things inside the White House itself were relatively calm. For the first time in years, Van Buren was leading a life centered on home and family. In fact, the White House was the first real home Van Buren had lived in since he entered politics.

For years Van Buren had been living for part of the year in Washington hotels, getting home to New York for only a few weeks at a time. Traveling had made him a regular guest at hotels and inns, places he later admitted that he detested. His sons had been living with relatives since their mother's death because Van Buren's living arrangements did not enable him to have the boys with him. Now, however, he had a large home to offer to his sons, and as soon as Van Buren was inaugurated, his sons Abraham, John, Smith, and Martin, Jr., joined him in the White House.

Mrs. Madison Makes a Match

The only thing the Van Buren White House lacked was a First Lady. Because Van Buren had never remarried, he had no wife to serve in the traditional role of White House hostess. Instead, Van Buren himself acted as the host on state occasions, personally attending to all the details his First Lady would otherwise have overseen.

Although Van Buren was well known for his social graces, many people thought it was inappropriate for the White House to be without a hostess. One of these people was Dolley Madison, the wife of former President James Madison and a prominent Washington hostess herself. Mrs. Madison decided to dedicate herself to finding a hostess for the President.

Angelica Singleton was introduced to President Van Buren and his family by former First Lady Dolley Madison. After she married Abraham Van Buren, the President's eldest son, Angelica became White House hostess. (Library of Congress.)

Van Buren himself had no desire to remarry; indeed, he had no time to think about such things, given all his duties as President. Therefore, Mrs. Madison concentrated on the President's sons, all of whom were now grown men. Since the tradition of the day was for children to marry according to their birth order (that is, the oldest would marry first, the youngest last), Mrs. Madison decided to find a mate for Abraham Van Buren, the President's eldest son.

One evening, Mrs. Madison brought a young woman from South Carolina with her to a White House dinner. Angelica Singleton was the daughter of a wealthy land owner, and she was beautiful. Abraham Van Buren was immediately taken with her, and she with him. Within a few months, the two were married.

Although the Van Buren family had a long tradition of marrying within its Dutch heritage, the President was nonetheless fond of his new daughter-in-law, who was of English extraction. Angelica soon became the President's hostess, fulfilling Dolley Madison's dream of adding a woman's touch to the Van Buren White House.

A Loyal Cabinet

The peaceful life in Van Buren's family quarters was matched in the Oval Office as well. Although he had many difficult problems to deal with during his term, Van Buren made sure he was surrounded by a loyal group of advisors.

Van Buren had been dismayed by the chaos that had marked Andrew Jackson's Cabinet (even though much of it had been Van Buren's own doing). The President did not want to endure the resignations and disloyalty that Jackson had suffered during the Eaton Affair. Therefore, he rewarded those who had been loyal to him.

By the end of Jackson's term, his Cabinet consisted of those advisors who had refused to join John C. Calhoun in his vendetta against Van Buren and Jackson. Van Buren kept these men for his own Cabinet. One of the most loyal of all was Attorney General Benjamin F. Butler, whom Van Buren had persuaded Jackson to appoint. Butler was the same man Van Buren had taken in as an apprentice in his law practice years before. The two had since become law partners, and Butler had served a term in the New York House of Representatives. Butler performed much the same function for Van Buren that Van Buren had served for Jackson—he acted as the President's closest advisor and as head of his Kitchen Cabinet.

Van Buren also got a lot of help and loyalty from his sons. John served as White House secretary, overseeing his father's schedule and helping him with his correspondence. And Abraham occasionally appeared before Congress in his father's place to deliver speeches for the President. The help of his sons and loyal advisors was vital to Van Buren during the many dark days of his term.

THE "LOG CABIN AND HARD CIDER" CAMPAIGN

In 1840 Martin Van Buren decided to seek a second term as President of the United States. For Van Buren it was an easy decision. For the Democrats, however, it was not. Van Buren had been under constant attack throughout his term, and the Democratic Party had taken a beating in local elections as a result. Nevertheless, the party nominated Van Buren for a second term when it met for its national convention in Baltimore in May. Needing a scapegoat of some kind, however, the party refused to renominate Vice-President Richard M. Johnson.

Van Buren's opponent in the presidential race was the same man he had opposed in 1836, William Henry Harrison of the Whig Party. From the beginning, Harrison waged a fierce campaign. As he had in the previous election, Harrison concentrated on attacking Van Buren and playing up his own war record.

Harrison was a retired Army general and a hero of the War of 1812. He was most famous for driving the American Indians out of the area that is now the states of Indiana, Michigan, and Illinois. In 1811 Harrison attacked the Indian village of Shawnee on the Tippecanoe River, earning him the nickname, "Old Tippecanoe." During the election campaign, the Whigs used the slogan "Tippecanoe and Tyler, too," to describe Harrison and his vice-presidential running mate, John Tyler.

Beyond slogans, Harrison's camp claimed that Van Buren had been callous to the needs of those Americans who had been hurt by the Panic of 1837. They accused him of throwing lavish White House parties and buying expensive, tailored clothes while his constituents could not afford to feed themselves. These charges were not accurate. Van Buren actually gave few parties at the White House, and although he was always fashionably dressed, his clothes cost no more than any other politician's.

Despite the fact that many of his charges were untrue, Harrison was successful in painting himself as a man of the people and Van Buren as a heartless aristocrat. Ironically, some of Van Buren's supporters unwittingly helped Harrison in his cause. The campaign became known as the "Log Cabin and Hard Cider" campaign after a pro-Van Buren newspaper printed an editorial attacking Harrison as a man who would give up his campaign and "spend his days in a log cabin" if given $2,000 and a barrel of hard cider (an alcoholic beverage made from fermented apples). Harrison used this attack to his advantage, claiming that his American hard cider was better than the expensive French wine Van Buren was said to consume.

One bright spot during this hard-fought campaign came on July 4, when Van Buren was able to sign his long-postponed Subtreasury Bill. But even as the President celebrated his success, Harrison was attacking the bill as a grave mistake. Apparently, many people agreed. When election results from around the nation were tallied on December 2, 1840, William Henry Harrison was declared the winner by an overwhelming majority. When the electoral college cast its votes to officially elect the President, Van Buren won just 60 votes to Harrison's 234.

Chapter 8
Free Soil and Hard Times

His humiliating defeat in the election of 1840 might have made Martin Van Buren a bitter man. His opponents had attacked his very character and had all but destroyed his reputation. Van Buren, however, was not a man who would allow his public dealings to invade his personal feelings. To show President-elect William Henry Harrison that he bore him no ill will, Van Buren invited Harrison to the White House a few weeks before the inauguration, setting a precedent that subsequent Presidents also have followed.

Van Buren's ability to separate politics from his personal life allowed him to befriend some of his fiercest political enemies after he left the White House. Henry Clay, the Whig senator who had violently opposed Van Buren's subtreasury plan and who had campaigned vigorously for Harrison in 1840, became a close associate of Van Buren's afterward. Van Buren respected Clay for refusing to engage in the dirty politics of many other Whigs. The two men corresponded with each other for the rest of their lives.

RETURN TO KINDERHOOK

The day after President Harrison was inaugurated, Martin Van Buren set out for Kinderhook. The thousands of well-wishers who lined Van Buren's route home proved that his reputation had not been utterly destroyed. When he stopped in New York City for a reception at City Hall, the place was overrun with more than 8,000 friends and supporters. Although he had lost New York to Harrison in the election, Van Buren remarked that he was nevertheless glad to be home.

When he arrived in Kinderhook, Van Buren found the town very much as he had left it. There was one major difference between the Kinderhook of 40 years before and the town that Van Buren returned to in 1841, however. This time, Martin Van Buren himself would occupy one of the stately mansions that he had only dreamed of in his youth.

The Master of Lindenwald

Van Buren took up residence in a large house known as Lindenwald. Ironically, the house had once belonged to Peter Van Ness, the patriarch of the Van Ness family and the man who had challenged Van Buren's right to vote in 1804. Now a wealthy man whose accomplishments had outstripped those of any of Kinderhook's former leaders, Van Buren relished his new-found position as the town's most powerful man.

The first thing Van Buren did when he returned to Kinderhook was to enlarge the already spacious Lindenwald. He added a tall Italian-style tower onto the rear of the house; from the tower's open balcony, one could see much of Kinderhook. He also added a large, formal entrance porch. When Van Buren was finished, the 36-room estate made a perfect home for him, his four sons and their wives, and his many grandchildren.

A Place in History for Lindenwald

The homes of many U.S. Presidents are so well known that almost any American can match them to the leader who lived there. Mount Vernon, almost everyone knows, was George Washington's home. Monticello is immediately recognized as Thomas Jefferson's estate. But few people recognize the name Lindenwald, Martin Van Buren's country home in his native Kinderhook, New York.

Van Buren purchased the home in 1839, while he was serving his term as President. He planned to retire to Lindenwald after the end of his second term, which would have been in 1845. However, because he was defeated by William Henry Harrison in the election of 1840, Van Buren retired to Lindenwald in 1841, four years earlier than planned.

Because Van Buren's political fortunes dwindled so dramatically in the years following his defeat, few people considered Lindenwald an important historic site. After Van Buren's death in 1862, much of his furniture was auctioned off, and Lindenwald itself was sold.

Over the next 100 years, Lindenwald became home to one family after another. In the early 1900s it was sold again, becoming a tea house. In the 1950s, it served as a nursing home. By the 1970s, the house was abandoned and had fallen into disrepair.

In 1973, however, new interest in Van Buren's presidency as well as in early-American architecture led the U.S. National

Park Service to take a look at Lindenwald. Because the Park Service's board of governors decided that Lindenwald was indeed an important part of American history, it was designated a public historic site. The Park Service then assigned a team of architects and historians the task of restoring Lindenwald to its original condition.

Restoring the house was a big challenge, because the Park Service has very strict rules for such restoration. For example, only furniture that belonged to the President while he was living in the house could be displayed. This meant that the Park Service had to track down and purchase furniture that had been sold more than 100 years before. (One important furnishing, Van Buren's bathtub, was found in a ditch behind the house.)

The Park Service also insisted that the carpeting and wallpaper had to be as much like the original as possible. Researchers had to examine old photographs and paintings of Lindenwald, and peel through layers of wallpaper and flooring, to find out what the house looked like in Van Buren's day.

In 1988 Lindenwald was opened to the public as a national historic site. The Park Service claims that the house looks almost exactly as it did when Van Buren lived there. According to one Park Service official, a walk through Lindenwald is a short biography of its famous owner's life. "We're telling the story of Martin Van Buren," the official said.

An Active Politician

Van Buren was not content simply to lounge around Lindenwald and enjoy family life, however. He was a born politician, and he soon decided to become involved in politics once again. Van Buren began renewing his contacts with members of the Democratic Party in New York, and he found that his old political skills had not forsaken him. He quickly regained much of his political power. By 1842 he was convinced that he could win the Democratic nomination for President in the election of 1844.

Van Buren decided to enhance his chances by taking a trip to the South, where his political fortunes were at their weakest. Although he claimed the purpose of the trip was to visit his aging mentor, Andrew Jackson, in Tennessee, Van Buren made sure he stopped in Kentucky as well. There, Van Buren visited Henry Clay, who was planning on seeking the Whig nomination in 1844. Agreeing that they would most probably be facing one another in the upcoming election, both men promised to fight fair. They also agreed to keep silent on the question of annexation of Texas, a subject on which neither man wanted to commit himself.

By 1844 most political observers agreed that Martin Van Buren would be the Democratic Party's candidate in the presidential race. A few months before the Democrat's national nominating convention, however, Van Buren's enemies in the South confronted him on the annexation issue. The southerners had obtained a letter written by Andrew Jackson recommending immediate annexation of Texas, and they called on Van Buren to either support or refute his old mentor.

As soon as he received the challenge, Van Buren contacted Henry Clay again. Clay assured Van Buren that he had nothing to do with introducing the issue into the campaign, and even agreed to publish a statement opposing annexation. In fact, both Van Buren and Clay published letters stating that they would oppose annexation of Texas if they were elected to the presidency.

Van Buren's public opposition to annexation pleased few Democrats, least of all Andrew Jackson. A southerner himself, the former President favored statehood for Texas because he wanted the South to have more influence in Congress. When he heard of Van Buren's opposition, a furious Jackson threw his support behind James Knox Polk, a congressman from Jackson's native Tennessee who was also seeking the Democratic presidential nomination.

Adding to Van Buren's woes was his old enemy, John C. Calhoun, who was himself trying to win the Democratic nomination. Calhoun tried to take advantage of the rift between Van Buren and Jackson by announcing his own unqualified support for annexation of Texas.

The Democrats Nominate a Candidate

When the Democrats gathered in Baltimore for their national convention, Van Buren believed he would get the nomination. Calhoun had failed to win many votes. Moreover, he could never hope to win the support of Jackson, who still resented Calhoun for his behavior while he was serving as Jackson's Vice-President. Van Buren's only real threat, therefore, was Polk, and Van Buren was confident that his years of experience would outweigh Jackson's endorsement of Polk. Before the convention began, Van Buren knew that he had secured the votes of more than half of the states at the convention.

Unfortunately for Van Buren, however, the Democrats enacted a new rule stating that a candidate needed a two-thirds majority of the votes to win the nomination. Although Van

Buren tried to have this rule changed, he was unsuccessful. After several ballots failed to give either candidate the necessary two-thirds majority, Van Buren's home state of New York switched its votes to Polk. The battle was over, and Van Buren had lost.

When the election was held in November, Polk defeated Henry Clay, the Whig candidate, to become the 11th President of the United States. After he took office in March 1845, Polk offered Van Buren the post of minister to Great Britain, but Van Buren refused. The Fox of Kinderhook suspected that Polk was simply trying to get him out of the country so that Polk could annex Texas without having to face the opposition of one of the Democratic Party's most powerful men. Van Buren's suspicions were proved accurate in July, when Polk succeeded in getting Congress to annex Texas.

POLITICIAN TURNED CRUSADER

The election of 1844 and its aftermath, particularly the annexation of Texas, effectively destroyed Martin Van Buren's power within the Democratic Party. Realizing that Van Buren's days as a party leader were over, many of his closest associates threw their support behind the Polk administration. Even Benjamin F. Butler, Van Buren's former law partner and the attorney general in Van Buren's administration, accepted a post in the Polk Cabinet.

Nevertheless, Martin Van Buren was not yet ready to give up politics. Nor was he ready to accept the spread of slavery in the United States that had been brought about by the annexation of Texas, a slave state. Now that he had nothing to lose, Van Buren was free to express his true thoughts on slavery, and he began to speak out loudly against it.

With the help of his son John, Van Buren began organiz-

Van Buren's vice-presidential running mate on the Free Soil ticket was Charles F. Adams, son of former President John Quincy Adams. The pair finished a poor third in the general election. As a result, Van Buren's political career came to an end. (Library of Congress.)

ing an antislavery faction of the Democratic Party. The faction was considered extremely radical, and many could not believe that an old loyal Democrat like Van Buren would try to fragment the party. Nevertheless, many like-minded party members joined Van Buren's group.

The Free Soil Democrats

The antislavery group soon became known as the Free Soil Democrats. Their enemies called them the Barnburners, claiming that they were willing to "burn down the barn to get rid of the rats"—that is, destroy the Union to get rid of slavery. Van Buren had no intention of destroying the Union; in fact, he felt that abolishing slavery was the only way to save the Union. Nor did he have any intention of destroying the Democratic Party. Rather, he hoped that his Free Soil Democrats would be able to convince the leadership of the Democratic Party to include an antislavery platform at their next national convention.

In 1848 the Democrats met again in Baltimore to nominate a presidential candidate. Much to the chagrin of the Free Soil faction, the Democrats nominated Lewis Cass of Michigan for President. Cass, who was against abolishing slavery, got the Democrats to draft a platform criticizing efforts to bring the question of slavery before Congress.

Because the Democrats refused to refute slavery in their platform, the Free Soil faction split from the Democrats and formed their own party. On July 9, 1848, the Free Soil Party held a convention in Buffalo, New York, to nominate their own candidate for President of the United States.

The Free Soil convention attracted some very important northern politicians, including Salmon P. Chase of Ohio and Charles Sumner of Massachusetts. The most important man there, however, was Martin Van Buren, who was unanimously nominated for President. The man chosen as Van Buren's vice-presidential running mate was Charles Francis Adams, the son of former President John Quincy Adams. No one failed to notice the irony in the fact that Van Buren was running with the son of one of his former archenemies.

The convention produced a platform calling for an end to slavery, free homesteads to settlers in the West, and improvements in roads and other public works. It also adopted a campaign slogan: "Free soil, free speech, free labor, and free men."

The Election of 1848

The Free Soil Party was not the only group that was formed in 1848 to protest slavery and nominate its own candidate. Another group, the Liberty League, was formed for the same purpose on June 2, 1848, at a meeting in Rochester, New York. The Liberty League nominated Gerrit Smith of New York as its presidential candidate, and Smith's candidacy was supported later that month by labor organizations at a meeting in Philadelphia.

Thus, even before he began to campaign for the 1848 election, Martin Van Buren was facing formidable odds. Not only was he up against the nation's two most powerful political parties, the Democrats and the Whigs, but he was competing with someone else for the votes of abolitionists (people who wanted to abolish slavery). Nevertheless, the 66-year-old Van Buren campaigned vigorously, giving his speeches with what one biographer later called "holy zeal."

Van Buren's zeal was not enough to counter the opposition, however. He received only 300,000 votes in the election—he had lost his re-election bid in 1840 after getting more than one million votes. Moreover, Van Buren's candidacy had drained votes away from the Democrats, helping Whig candidate Zachary Taylor, a slaveowner, to win the election.

A PRIVATE CITIZEN AT LAST

The election of 1848 forever ended Martin Van Buren's active involvement in politics. Although he retained his antislavery sentiments throughout the rest of his life, Van Buren dedicated his remaining years to travel, family, and reflection.

In 1852, after his old friend, General Winfield Scott, was defeated in the presidential election by Franklin Pierce, Van Buren went to Europe. After visiting friends in London, he traveled to his family's native Holland, where he visited the towns in which his Dutch ancestors had lived. As the first former American President ever to visit Europe, Van Buren was greeted with affection and respect everywhere he went. And as an American of Dutch ancestry, he was given especially warm treatment in Holland.

From Holland, Van Buren traveled to Italy, where, in 1854, he settled in the city of Sorrento. There, in the company of his son and namesake, Martin, Jr., Van Buren began to work on his autobiography. Historians would later note that Van Buren's memory of events was very selective—the manuscript makes little mention of some of his more controversial actions. However, Van Buren died before he could complete his autobiography, and it was never published.

In 1856, after the death of Martin, Jr., Van Buren returned to Kinderhook. Some members of New York's Democratic Party tried to induce Van Buren to reactivate his political career, but the aging former President was not interested. He even refused to attend a Democratic dinner in New York City, complaining that the party had completely lost its dedication to the ideals of Thomas Jefferson.

Van Buren's last political act occurred in 1860, when he publicly endorsed Abraham Lincoln for President. Lincoln was the candidate of the Republican Party, which had been formed by many of the abolitionists who had supported the

John Van Buren, the President's second and favorite son, was one of his father's most trusted advisors. John later rose to prominence in New York politics, serving as a leader of the New York bar. When President Van Buren retired to Kinderhook, John and his brothers took up residence at Lindenwald. (Library of Congress.)

Free Soil Party in 1848. Van Buren was convinced that only the Republicans could save the Union. However, it is doubtful that the support of the aging and feeble Van Buren had any substantial impact on the election, which Lincoln won.

For the next two years, Van Buren remained in Kinderhook. By 1862 he was so weak that he rarely left his second-floor bedroom at Lindenwald. On July 24, 1862, at the age of 79, Martin Van Buren died. He was buried in Kinderhook alongside his beloved Hannah.

Chapter 9
The Van Buren Legacy

Martin Van Buren was not one of those Presidents who achieved immortality. Unlike Washington, Lincoln, or Kennedy, he remains an obscure figure to most Americans, his administration all but lost to history.

Many other Presidents share Van Buren's obscure fate. Despite their accomplishments, their achievements and opinions have been clouded by those of men such as Jefferson, Jackson, and the Roosevelts, men who made deeper and more lasting marks on the national record. Like them, Van Buren achieved much that has lived long after him, and even those who have forgotten him are familiar with the many fruits of his political career.

A MAN OF ACCOMPLISHMENT

Martin Van Buren was active in politics for almost 50 years, from the moment he attended his first political convention in 1800 until his final presidential campaign in 1848. During that time, he helped to mold the political direction and shape the public policy of a young and fragile Union.

This rare photograph of Martin Van Buren was taken around 1850, after he had retired from politics. The former President spent his final years traveling throughout Europe and writing his memoirs. (Library of Congress.)

Some of the things that Martin Van Buren left behind have not won him many admirers. He was the first American politician to create and employ a "political machine," a powerful organization capable of gaining absolute control over the politics of a city or state. He was also the first politician to openly use political patronage on the national level, hiring and firing federal employees solely on the basis of their political affiliations. And it was Van Buren who, during Andrew Jackson's administration, formed the first Kitchen Cabinet, a group of presidential advisors that exercised more influence over national policy than did the President's official Cabinet. Many people believe that Van Buren's memory is tarnished by his role in introducing such dubious systems into the national political arena.

Other Van Buren accomplishments are clearly more positive, however. He was the first President to recognize the need for an independent national treasury, which now forms the basis of the U.S. monetary system. Along with Andrew Jackson, he was one of the founders of the Democratic Party and served as its standard-bearer for many of its early years. And he successfully avoided a series of wars during his presidency, sparing the country much bloodshed.

Martin Van Buren lived through and participated in many of the most important events of his time. Born just five days after the signing of the peace treaty that ended the American Revolution, Van Buren lived through the Whiskey Rebellion, the War of 1812, the seige of the Alamo, and the attack on Fort Sumter that started the Civil War (he died before the war ended). He played an active part in the Erie Canal, the Indian War, the Panic of 1837, and the abolitionist movement.

Many of Van Buren's presidential "firsts" have long been forgotten. He was the first President born under the American flag (the first born after the signing of the Declaration of Independence), the first New Yorker elected to the presidency, and the first President whose predecessor actively campaigned for him. These and other facts about Van Buren are now being rediscovered as historians begin to take a closer look at his presidency and his legacy. More than 100 years after his death, the Fox of Kinderhook is beginning to resume his place as one of the most important figures in the history of the United States.

Bibliography

Curtis, James C. *The Fox at Bay: Martin Van Buren and the Presidency, 1837–1841*. Lexington, Kentucky: University Press of Kentucky, 1970. Written by a noted history professor, this book shows how Van Buren's term in office marked an important period of transition for the presidency, from a relatively weak office controlled by Congress to the strong position it is today.

Hargrove, Jim. *Martin Van Buren*. Chicago: Childrens Press, 1987. This brief but complete account of Van Buren's life and presidency was written especially for young readers. It includes a chronology of American history and many illustrations.

Hoyt, Edwin P. *Martin Van Buren*. Chicago: Reilly & Lee, 1964. Hoyt, who has written many histories and biographies for younger readers, believes that Van Buren was the first true "political animal" to emerge from American democracy. This book emphasizes the "wheeling and dealing" that earned Van Buren the nickname "The Little Magician."

Niven, John. *Martin Van Buren: The Romantic Age of American Politics*. New York and Oxford: Oxford University Press, 1983. This book, considered to be the most complete biography ever written about Van Buren, is an in-depth study of the man and the era in which he lived. Special attention is given to the other politicians of the Romantic Age, including Aaron Burr, John C. Calhoun, and Andrew Jackson.

Remini, Robert V. *Martin Van Buren and the Making of the Democratic Party*. New York: Columbia University Press, 1959. Remini discusses Van Buren's contribution to creating the Democratic Party, following his career from his early involvement with the Democratic-Republicans through his term as the nation's second Democratic President.

Shepard, Edward M. *Martin Van Buren*. Boston and New York: Houghton, Mifflin, 1899. Written less than 40 years after Van Buren's death, this book tells the story of Van Buren's life and presidency from a 19th-century perspective. The author defends Van Buren against the charge that he was a political manipulator with no strong moral principles.

Wilson, Major L. *The Presidency of Martin Van Buren*. Lawrence, Kansas: University Press of Kansas, 1984. Wilson looks closely at the issues Van Buren faced during his years in the White House, including the Panic of 1837 and the question of slavery.

Index